Fat, Drunk, and Stupid

Also by Matty Simmons

On the House (with Don Simmons)
The Diners Club Drink Book
The Best: Collection of Short Stories
The Card Castle (A Novel)
*If You Don't Buy This Book, We'll Kill This Dog: Life, Laughs,
        Love and Death at* National Lampoon
The Credit Card Catastrophe

Fat, Drunk, and Stupid

THE INSIDE STORY BEHIND THE MAKING
OF *ANIMAL HOUSE*

Matty Simmons

ST. MARTIN'S PRESS ✖ NEW YORK

All photos courtesy of Universal City Studio, LLC, except photo of Richard
Lariviere, courtesy of the University of Oregon

Excerpts on pages 38 and 183 from *The Real Animal House* by Chris Miller. Used
by permission of the author.

Excerpt on pages 209–210 from a *Huffington Post* article by Sean Daniel. Used by
permission of the author.

Excerpt on pages 211–213 from AMCtv.com article by Christine Fall, copyright
© 2010–2011 American Movie Classics Company, LLC. All rights reserved.

Excerpt on pages 213–214 from "Old School" by Michael Simmons, as originally
published in *LA Weekly*. Used courtesy of the author.

www.stmartins.com

Library of Congress Cataloging-in-Publication Data

Simmons, Matty.
    Fat, drunk, and stupid : the inside story behind the making of
Animal house / Matty Simmons.—1st ed.
        p. cm.
    ISBN 978-0-312-55226-8 (hardcover)
    ISBN 978-1-4299-4235-5 (e-book)
    1. Animal house (Motion picture)   I. Title.
    PN1997.A4255S57 2012
    791.43—dc23
                                            2011046556

First Edition: April 2012

10   9   8   7   6   5   4   3   2

This book is dedicated to

Doug Kenney,
John Belushi,
and John Vernon,

You lit up the "House"

In Appreciation

I wrote this book with a lot of help from friends and colleagues, who told me about things I didn't remember and other stories and events I'd never heard before. Making a movie like *Animal House* brings you close to everybody else associated with it; I guess it's the pride we all share.

I thank my wife and partner, Patti, who has always told me straight-out when she thought I had gone off track.

And then there's my oldest daughter, Julie Simmons-Lynch, who worked long hours and days and months trying to translate her old man's memories into something comprehensible. Since I write with pen and tape recorder, I'm sure there were times when she doubted that English is my first and only language.

Much appreciation to my literary agent, Paul Bresnick, who has done battle for me when battle was called for and told me I was wrong when that was required.

I have written six books before this and worked with six

really good editors but no one who was so on target, so frequently right, and so committed as Yaniv Soha. I thank him.

And with much appreciation to Sean Daniel and Thom Mount, the studio executives who knew a good thing when they saw it . . . and fought for it.

Contents

Contents

Preface

Before *Animal House*, I had produced theatre for years, going back to high school and the army, where I was in charge of entertainment. At the *National Lampoon* we had, by 1976, produced a number of successful comedy revues, a radio show, and comedy albums. That year, I decided that we were going to make a movie. We had a writing team and, finally, a 114-page treatment that was as tasteless and disorderly and akin to the *National Lampoon* magazine as any movie treatment the folks in Hollywood had ever seen.

Was it a good idea, a good treatment?

Was the world ready for a film based on *National Lampoon* humor?

Well, sometimes you're wrong.

And sometimes you're right.

The late Billy Wilder, one of the great screenwriters and directors in the history of film, once met with the legendary studio boss Sam Goldwyn and pitched him a story. "It's about the great ballet dancer Nijinsky," he explained, and went on to tell Nijinsky's story, which ends with him going crazy and thinking that he's a horse. Goldwyn listened blankly, and then threw up his arms, gesturing wildly. "Do you think I'm nuts?" he asked. "I should do a movie about a ballet dancer, and one who goes crazy and thinks he's a horse?"

Wilder thought for a moment, then said, "What if I change the ending and he wins the Kentucky Derby?"

Nobody ever did Wilder's story. Rumor has it that Nijinsky is still pulling a carriage in Central Park.

Somehow, miraculously, *Animal House was* made.

This book tells the story.

1

THE HOUSE IS OPEN

It was July 26, 1978, a hot and humid Friday night. I drove down Park Avenue slowly—everyone and everything moved slowly. The car in front of me seemed not to move at all. The people in the streets didn't walk with the usual New York over-drive but with the tired tread of a weary and almost defeated populace. It was summer in Manhattan and one of those nights that you think of only as an excuse to go to the mountains or the beach, or anywhere where you can breathe.

It seemed I was the only one on Park Avenue whose adrenaline was pumping. I was a nervous wreck and the crawl of everything surrounding me aggravated me even more. I turned left on 57th Street and drove slowly to the Sutton Theatre, just east of Third Avenue. Now, the street was crowded and people were moving briskly. I crossed over Third and stared at the crowd in front of the theatre. The ticket line stretched all the way to Second Avenue and beyond. It was not unlike that at a rock concert, with hundreds of people—primarily young, screaming, running, laughing, calling to each other, and waiting on line. It was the line for the 6 P.M. showing on opening day of *National Lampoon*'s *Animal House*.

A kid in his late teens ran by me and yelled to a friend, "They're sold out until the midnight show and we have to get on line." I looked at my watch. It was 5:50.

I remembered what Charlie Powell had told me. A week earlier we had screened the movie at the American Book Association convention in Atlanta. The place was jammed with 10,000 people for the book fair and to see an advance showing of this new film. I was upset. The sound of the movie was not recorded for an arena. Fifteen minutes into the film I got up and strode out into the lobby. I just stood there alone, smoking, and trying to listen to the reactions from the audience. Charlie then marketing head of Universal Studios, saw me and came over. I told him I was disturbed because the sound was so bad. He smiled and put a hand on my shoulder. "You've got nothing to worry about, Matty," he said. "I swear on my son's life that you have a major hit." I'd never heard anyone take such an oath, then I turned and saw that behind him was Buddy Young, Universal's public relations director. He'd heard what Charlie said, laughed, and said, " You're in good shape, Matty. Charlie loves his son very much."

"A major hit," he had said. And now I could see from the lines at the Sutton theater that Charlie might be right.

At eight o'clock I drove to the Loews theater on 86th Street. It was the same scene, lines around the block. Then I moved across to Broadway to the Astor, where a few days before we'd held the world premiere of the film. There were at least 2,000 people on lines around the block. Not stopping on Broadway, I drove back to the Sutton and sat in my car until the ten o'clock show. The lines were again snaking around 57th Street to Third Avenue. As I looked around the crowd, I noticed a familiar figure standing quietly watching. It was Walter Garibaldi, the assistant to the treasurer of the *National Lampoon*, and in his hand was a small calculator, which he kept tapping. I called out his name and he walked over to my car. "What the hell are you doing?" I asked. He smiled and told me, "I'm just figuring out how much money we make every time somebody buys a ticket." Later that evening, when I returned, Walter was still there, three crushed coffee cups at his feet, still tapping numbers into his little calculator.

In Chicago that night, *Lampoon* editor John Hughes sat alone in a jammed movie theater watching the film. He'd stood in line for a half hour or so to get in. When the picture ended, he later told me, "I said to myself, I'm going to make movies."

Universal executive Sean Daniel and the distribution people were calling studio head Ned Tanen to give him numbers and tell him about the opening-day reaction to *Animal House*.

At one point, Tanen called Universal chairman Lew Wasserman and told him what was going on. Wasserman thought about it for a moment and mused, "Funny how such a little movie can turn out to be such a big movie." A few years earlier, the same thing had happened at Universal with the low-budget *American Graffiti*, but it appeared that this was going to be even bigger. And it was.

Tanen, Sid Sheinberg, president of MCA, Universal's parent company, and Wasserman phoned each other constantly over the weekend, getting day-by-day box office reports and congratulating each other.

Universal had agreed to have the world premiere in New York City and asked me to run it. My staff and I were to handle the invitations and to set up the premiere party. I gathered everybody who worked on the business end of the *Lampoon* in my office. We would invite, of course, key members of the cast and crew, Universal officials, celebrities, the magazine's advertisers, and the staff of 21st Century Communications, the parent company of the *Lampoon*. My assistant, Barbara Atti, would coordinate the event. From the start, I knew I wanted to have the party at the Village Gate. Its two floors could house 2,000 guests and it had been the place where we kicked off our first live show, *National Lampoon's Lemmings*, in 1973. It was this play that featured John Belushi, Chevy Chase, Christopher Guest, and others.

Guests were asked to wear college garb: anything that they might have worn, or thought about wearing, during their days at college. Some came in togas, others in T-shirts or letter sweaters, carrying pennants from their alma maters. Belushi wore the famous "COLLEGE" sweatshirt. There were girls in cheerleader costumes and a couple of guys came in football uniforms. Some came as Bluto look-alikes.

I wanted servers everywhere with trays of food, and I wanted college-kid food: hot dogs, hamburgers, and snacks of every kind. There would be no hard liquor, just kegs of beer. Sixties rock bands would play wall-to-wall music. It was spectacular, and I remember it all so well, even though it was one of the few times in my life when I spent an evening in what seemed to be a total daze.

The screening of the film that night started with a problem. The movie was supposed to begin at 7 P.M. By that time, the Astor theater was jammed with 3,000 people. We had to rent another theater some blocks north to screen the film for the overflow crowd. The audience was getting restless at the Astor. We were waiting because John Landis, the film's director, was late. At 7:25 he still hadn't arrived and I told my assistant to tell the projectionist to start. I was too restless to sit and watch the movie, so, again, I stood out in the lobby. At 7:30 Landis and costume designer Deborah Nadoolman, whom he later married, came dashing in. He was furious that the movie was already screening and began arguing with me in the lobby. Both of us threatened to start throwing punches. We were face to face when Universal execs Thom Mount and Sean Daniel moved between us and separated us. Landis then went into the theater and watched the rest of the film while sitting on the steps of the balcony. His reserved seats had been taken.

Down at the Village Gate on Bleecker Street, Barbara Atti and her crew were set. Every entrance to the Gate was guarded, not only by uniform police but by the senior class of Columbia Prep, headed by my son Andy, a senior there at the time. I had first done something like that at the after-party for the opening of *Lemmings* when my older son Michael's Horace Mann senior class guarded the entrance, so that only those with invitations would be allowed into Minetta Tavern on MacDougal Street. Now it was the Village Gate and we expected ten times the crowd that had been invited to the *Lemmings* party. We invited 2,000 people; more than 5,000 showed up, some with, more without, invitations. So there was a 3,000-seat world premiere, a 1,000-seat theater in addition, and then a 2,000-plus party. Thousands of people contacted us to get an invitation to the premiere and the party. Crashers were stopped by the guards, who looked like a small army surrounding the Pentagon. Warner Bros.' chief Steve Ross came by. Ross put a hand on my shoulder. "I guess," he said, "we should have made the movie at Warner." (Steve, in the course of his career, had gone from Riverside Funeral Home in New York, to Kinney Parking, merged it with Independent News Company, and then acquired Warner Bros. His company would eventually merge with Time, Inc., creating Time Warner.)

The music at the party was nonstop. Groups like Joey Dee and the Starliters played sixties classics. At one point, the Michael Simmons Band played Stephen Bishop's theme song from *Animal House* and members of the cast jumped on stage and led the singing. As they sang, John Belushi leaped off the stage, raced to the back of the club, grabbed me, and partly pulled, partly carried me, onto the stage and I joined them.

Sean Daniel remembers the studio's response to the reaction to *Animal House* at the premiere screening and party. "I phoned Ned and he said to me—you know Ned had that dark, gloomy humor about him—'I know it's about to open, I know you've had good previews, but I still think you gotta choose which building you should jump off, the Chrysler or the Empire State

Building, you still got time to make that choice.' I said, 'Ned, we've been through so much, it's working! It's gonna work.' There was a part of Ned that was a rebel. Much of this movie appealed to him as a way of sticking it to the rest of the people because he always wanted to remind them how straight and uptight they were."

National Lampoon's *Animal House* became the number-one picture in America for eight weeks. It slid to second for two weeks, because of the prebooked Christmas movies and, remarkably, was brought back in February and became number one again. No other movie in recent motion picture history has ever had such a run. It became more than a movie. *Animal House* changed comedy, and attitudes, particularly among college audiences, where the movie became a prototype among young people.

Perhaps Roger Ebert described best the reaction to the film on college campuses in his *Chicago Sun-Times* article.

In the days and weeks and months and years that followed, life on college campuses had changed. Tim Matheson, as Otter, had said, "We can do anything we want, we're college students!" The words were taken literally, things changed. Whereas in the late '60s and early '70s college students stopped being "wild and crazy" and spent more time fighting against or for the war in Vietnam, they would now let loose and the trigger was *National Lampoon's Animal House*.

2

THE ROAD TO THE "HOUSE"

The Diners Club begat *Weight Watchers Magazine* which begat the *National Lampoon* and that begat *Animal House*.

When I was a very young press agent in 1949, handling mostly nightclubs and restaurants in New York City, I was approached by two men, a lawyer and a loan company executive, who had an idea. They invited me to their office and held up a card. On it was handwritten THE DINERS CLUB. The man who came up with the idea, Frank McNamara, told me you could go to restaurants and hotels and nightclubs all over New York City and charge your expenses, and then get one bill, once a month.

I had never charged anything in my life and couldn't imagine why anyone would not want to simply pay for everything with cash or check. McNamara insisted, he said people would love the convenience. I thought it over and a month or so later, McNamara's partner, Ralph E. Schneider, called me and asked if we could have lunch. He said they needed me.

They needed the publicity, but just as important they needed someone who had contacts in the restaurant and nightclub business. They'd heard that I handled publicity for more than a dozen leading clubs and dining places. The establishments they had approached didn't know them. The idea that the customer charged a meal on one day but the restaurants wouldn't be paid until the end of the month made them nervous. Now I was intrigued.

On February 8, 1950, McNamara, Schneider, and I walked downstairs to a restaurant called Major's Cabin Grill on New York's West 33rd Street, adjacent to the Empire State Building where their offices were located. We had lunch and when the tab came, McNamara handed the waiter The Diners Club card number 1,000. Schneider was carrying in his wallet number 1,001, and I had 1,002. The waiter, who had been given details about it earlier that day, accepted the card. This was the very first credit card charge. Within a year, The Diners Club had 100,000 cardholders in the New York area alone. Within two years we had become a public company, soon to go on the New York Stock Exchange. At that time, more than a million people throughout the United States were carrying the card.

Early on, I started *The Diners Club Magazine*, which would later segue into *Signature*, a publication that eventually had a circulation of more than 2 million. I became excited more about publishing than public relations. So much so that seventeen years later, when I resigned as executive vice president of the company, I decided to start my own publishing business.

In mid-1967, newspapers carried stories about my departure from The Diners Club and told of the new company I was about to start, 21st Century Communications. I met with Al Lippert, who had cofounded Weight Watchers with the original weight watcher herself, Jean Nidetch. It was like The Diners Club in its early years, a burgeoning new concept that would eventually become a public company. Lippert had read about my departure from The Diners Club and of my new company. He saw that I had taken a corporate publication and had turned it into a successful consumer's magazine, one that had general-interest features but also promoted the company. Would I do the same for *Weight Watchers Magazine*? I knew little about Weight Watchers but went to some meetings and met with Mrs. Nidetch, who impressed me tremendously. She was a powerful personality who spoke like a Baptist preacher, with thousands cheering her on when she lectured. I agreed to publish the magazine. It was launched in 1968 and became an instant success. My company owned half and Weight Watchers the other half. The profits from the magazine had us looking for other publishing properties. We experimented with a rock magazine that preceded the debut of *Rolling Stone* by four or five months. It was called *Cheetah*, named for a nightclub in New York. I knew little about contemporary music but tried to hire people who did. Soon I realized we had problems. It was the late sixties and nearly everybody on staff was on drugs. They would come to work in the middle of the day or not at all, they'd miss deadlines and fall asleep at their desks; the first editor I put in charge simply disappeared. *Cheetah* is still remembered by many for a pull-out poster of Mama Cass as a parody of a *Playboy* playmate. But finally we decided to close it down. The failure of *Cheetah* may very well have been a stroke of luck.

What happened soon after might not have happened if we'd stuck with it.

Weight Watchers Magazine continued to thrive, circulation exceeded a million, and we were still looking for more properties to publish. I had grown close to the people at Independent News Company. They were the distributors of our magazine, along with *Rolling Stone*, *Playboy*, and many others. The president of the company was Harold Chamberlain, a large, red-faced man with a great sense of humor and a love of liquor and poker. We started a weekly poker game that was held at my house every Wednesday night; nobody missed a game. We all became good friends. From the friendships struck at that poker table, a meeting would happen that would transform the way the world looked at comedy.

3

HARVARD ARRIVES

Harold called me one day. "I got some kids from Harvard here in my office," he said. He told me they belonged to the *Harvard Lampoon,* the iconic college humor magazine, and had written a parody of *Life* magazine that his company would soon distribute. The *Harvard Lampoon,* which regularly received sizeable donations from alumni, had financed the project and they were to go to press in the next couple of weeks. It had little national advertising and he wondered if I could help. I told him to send them over to my office, then at 1790 Broadway. On that afternoon, Doug Kenney, Henry Beard, and Rob Hoffman entered my office and my life.

The three of them reminded me of my best friend in high school, Howard Stein, who would go on to become the chairman of the board of the Dreyfus Company and the creator of the mutual fund. As a young man, Howard was incredibly impressive. He was handsome and personable and easily the smartest kid I had ever known. When I first met Kenney,

Beard, and Hoffman, I saw that they had the same articulate brightness, the same attractiveness, the same maturity at very young ages. Hoffman, the businessman of the group, was twenty-one; Kenney, the volatile, mad creator, was twenty-two; and Beard, the intellect, the deep thinker, was twenty-three. I have been told that at Harvard, Beard was considered the university's Bernard Baruch, the famed advisor to presidents and other world leaders. Beard, like Baruch, would often be found sitting on a bench, doing much of what Baruch was famous for, giving advice to all comers. He'd sit back, light his pipe, blow out some smoke, and simply say wise things.

At the time, I knew as little about the *Harvard Lampoon* as I had about Weight Watchers. I knew that many celebrated writers and humorists, and much of the great humor of the first part of the twentieth century, had come from those minds. I didn't knew much else, but my impression of the three young men who entered my office in 1968 was so indelibly etched in my mind that it has stayed with me all these years later. They told me what they planned to do and gave me some of the material that Beard and Kenney and others had written. Hoffman wasn't a humorist, he was the dealmaker of the group. And it was with Hoffman that I would eventually negotiate.

I took the material back to my office and Leonard Mogel—who had been the publisher of *Signature, The Diners Club Magazine* and had come with me from The Diners Club—and I looked them over. I learned that the *Harvard Lampoon* was composed not only of bright minds but of famous pedigrees. There was Christopher Cerf, whose father, Bennett Cerf, was the founder of Random House; John Weidman, whose father was the author and playwright Jerome Weidman. His play *I Can Get It for You Wholesale* introduced a young Barbra Streisand on Broadway. Playwright Moss Hart's son, Chris, was also a *Harvard Lampoon* contributor, as was Tim Crouse whose father, Russel, cowrote *Life with Father*, which at one time was the longest-running show on Broadway. The senior member of the group, George W.S. Trow, would later become a regular at *The New Yorker*, and his father was a well-known newspaper editor. It was an impressive group of contributors. The target of their humor was *Life* magazine, founded by Henry Luce and once one of the most widely read magazines in America but whose popularity had been fading and was slowly coming to the end of its weekly run.

Nonetheless, we agreed to help them. Mogel, who ran our advertising sales, sent his people out and they sold some national advertising. Independent News distributed the *Life* parody. In the end, however, it was a failure; the magazine lost the nearly $100,000 that the *Harvard Lampoon* had invested in it. But we were taken with the sheer talent involved. We knew there could be something meaningful in any association with them.

Together we came up with a new plan: another parody, this time targeting the much more popular *Time* magazine. We suspected that *Life* had simply been a bad choice. Picture magazines were becoming extinct because of television. *Time*, on the other hand, was a magazine of news and opinion and dealt in more subjects with more extensive coverage than television. And it had a huge circulation.

With the *Time* parody, the *Harvard Lampoon* made back

the entire investment it had lost with the *Life* parody, plus profits. And as all this was happening, my team and I were getting closer to these young men. While working on the *Time* parody we frequently sat around and talked about what to do next together. We came up with the idea of producing a national humor magazine.

No humor magazine for adults had existed successfully on a large scale in the United States since the early days of *The New Yorker*. There was *Mad*, of course, but it was more of a comic book, and while it was very popular, it didn't carry advertising and was aimed at teens. Hugh Hefner had published his humor magazine, *Trump*, but it lasted only a few issues. Other attempts failed as quickly.

In 1969, Rob Hoffman and I sat for days negotiating an agreement between the *Harvard Lampoon* and 21st Century and a second contract between 21st Century and Beard, Kenney, and Hoffman. We had already agreed that the new magazine would be called the *National Lampoon*. We sat for hours arguing, laughing, cursing, quibbling, and, finally, agreeing. 21st Century would put up all of the money and would have 75 percent ownership, and Beard, Kenney, and Hoffman would get 25 percent. The *Harvard Lampoon* would get a small percentage of magazine sales, though not advertising revenue. I would be chairman of the board and I'd be running the show.

4

THE *NATIONAL LAMPOON*

The first issue of the *National Lampoon* was dated April 1970. The humor was certainly there but I was unhappy with its direction—mostly with the look and organization of the magazine and its covers. After the fourth issue, I fired the art directors, wanting a slicker, more professional look. The one thing I didn't want was an underground magazine, so I hired award-winning art director Michael Gross. He, as much as Kenney and Beard, was responsible for the then sudden popularity of the *Lampoon*. We also added intriguing cover lines, and within a year circulation had gone into the high hundreds of thousands, and later in the decade over a million. It caught on, especially with young people, particularly those in college. And it caught on, too, with other humorists.

From the very first issue, *Harvard Lampoon* contributors such as Weidman, Cerf, and Trow came to work with Kenney and Beard. Soon after that others arrived: British comic Tony Hendra, Canadian Michel Choquette, Anne Beatts, who'd become the first female contributing editor to the *Lampoon*, and Chris Miller, whose short stories were the most popular of their genre in the magazine's twenty-year life. There was B. K. Taylor, Shary Flenniken, Gerald Sussman, Bruce McCall, Sean Kelly, Ed Subitzky, Vaughn Bodé, Gahan Wilson, Brian McConnachie, and P.J. O'Rourke, who started at the *Lampoon* as my assistant, then became an assistant editor, and eventually editor in chief. Perhaps most notable was Michael O'Donoghue, who went on to create the *National Lampoon Radio Hour* and then *Saturday Night Live*, where he was head writer for a number of years, using the same format and many of the same actors and writers as the *Radio Hour*. He would be joined or followed on the *Lampoon* staff by Jeff Greenfield, who went on to become a prominent television commentator; Al Jean and Michael Reiss, who would produce *The Simpsons*; Ed Bluestone, who conceived the now famous "If You Don't Buy this Magazine, We'll Shoot this Dog" *Lampoon* cover—one of the American Society of Magazine Editors top 40 magazine covers of all time—as well as those stories entitled "Telling a Kid His Parents Are Dead" and "Twenty-Three Ways to be Offensive at a Funeral of Someone You Didn't Like." In the late seventies, John Hughes, who would go on to become the most successful and prolific comedy screenwriter in the history of motion pictures, joined the staff. It was the greatest collection of humorists, over a twenty-year period, since perhaps the days of the Algonquin Round Table, when early Harvard humorists such as Robert Benchley, Alexander Woollcott, Dorothy Parker, and George S. Kaufman met almost daily while writing for film, stage, and magazines.

For nearly a decade the *Lampoon* was the second-biggest

selling publication on the newsstands, behind only *Cosmopolitan.* Bill Maher has said, "Without the *Lampoon* I would never have gotten through adolescence." In a recent interview, Jim Carrey said of a classic *Lampoon* comedy album, "We would smoke a joint and listen to *That's Not Funny, That's Sick* and all would be right with the world."

It was by far the biggest-selling magazine at college bookstores. In the seventies it was read by more than 1.2 million people a month. It ridiculed everybody and everything. It was fiercely antiwar and anti-know-nothings. It was intellectual but it was hot and saucy and sexy, and it was the first magazine that dared to say and do things that others hadn't before. It brought humor from the thirties and forties to the baby boomers. It introduced today's style of comedy. What you see on television and in movies today was first pioneered by the *National Lampoon.* Critics called it tasteless and juvenile, prompting O'Donoghue to suggest that "juvenile" was the liberal codeword for funny.

Breaking taboos wasn't without its costs. The magazine never got an automobile ad or ads from many other major companies. Nevertheless, it was highly profitable for years. The only rule at the *Lampoon* was that you could say anything you wanted to as long as it was redeemably funny. Most of the time it was.

As the magazine readership soared, what was happening in the editorial offices, now located at 635 Madison Avenue at 59th Street, in a posh Eastside building, was chaotic to say the least. At any one point, somebody wasn't talking to almost anybody else, particularly O'Donoghue, who first became Hendra's closest friend and then lashed out at him furiously when he discovered that Hendra had slept with his girlfriend.

O'Donoghue demanded I fire Hendra but I declined to get involved with the personal problems of the staff.

One member of the staff sleeping with the wife or girlfriend of another member actually wasn't all that unusual. Interestingly, O'Donoghue's girlfriend at the time was Amy Ephron, one of the well-known Hollywood Ephron sisters, who went on to become a studio executive and film producer. Years later, an accusation by Hendra's daughter that he had sexually abused her as a young girl was widely covered in the press.

Doug Kenney, during one of his many disappearances, just happened to take our assistant managing editor with him. We shall call her Mary Marshmallow, which is how she was addressed at the *Lampoon*. After a month or so she returned with him, went to her desk without saying a word, and resumed her work.

Scuttlebutt has it, that in the 80s one of the senior editors took a younger editor under his wing and wound up sleeping with the young man's wife. I will not go into any more detail but mention this only to show that refereeing the sexual peccadilloes of the *Lampoon* staff would have been a full-time job.

But there was also a special kind of camaraderie at the *National Lampoon*. Two stories might help describe it: Hendra decided that it would be good exercise for him to bike from his home in Greenwich Village to the midtown office of the *Lampoon* every day. The first time out, he collided with a little old lady on Park Avenue, was given a summons, and later was hit with a personal injury suit. The second day, he chained his bike to a street pole. When he came back that evening, only the handle of the bike and the chain remained. The staff, exhibiting typical *Lampoon* sympathy, chipped in and bought him a single skate, just one.

If there was no one at the *Lampoon* quite as colorful as Michael O'Donoghue, Ted Mann was close.

One day, I got an emergency call from Mann, who was in a phone booth in midtown. Apparently, he had locked himself in the booth after being pursued through the city streets by three large men whose obvious anger had indicated that they wanted to do damage to him. It seems, Ted had, like Hendra, decided to bike to work that day. En route, a car containing these three men had cut him off. In anger, Ted had pulled his bicycle chain out of the basket and smashed it against the car. A pursuit ensued. As they caught up to him, he dashed into a telephone booth and jammed it closed and started calling fellow editors for help.

When O'Rourke received a distress call from Mann, he assembled the editorial staff in his office and asked what they thought about all going down to rescue him. They took a vote. No one voted in favor of the rescue even though the phone booth imprisonment was only a few blocks from the office. *Lampoon* editors were lovers, not fighters. To them, showing camaraderie meant: Do something funny.

Unscathed, Mann finally arrived at the office carrying a mangled bicycle. He explained that he'd finally convinced his pursuers to take a check for the damages and had assured them that he would be here if for any reason the check didn't clear.

"Do you think," he asked me, "I could say I was on company business and get the *Lampoon*'s insurance company to pay me back?"

5

A BUSINESS LIKE SHOW BUSINESS

In the early 1970s, before their estrangement, O'Donoghue came to me and said he and Hendra had an idea to do a comedy album. From this came *National Lampoon's Radio Dinner*, our first venture outside the world of publishing. Once I embraced the idea of doing a comedy album, Gerald Taylor, who was publisher of the magazine at the time and had strong contacts in the recording industry, sold the deal to RCA Victor. RCA insisted on seeing all the material before it was recorded, but O'Donoghue, in particular, wouldn't stand for any censorship and refused to send them anything. After the recordings were made, RCA said that they wouldn't manufacture the albums until they heard the tapes. O'Donoghue relented and let them listen to what had been recorded. Immediately RCA said a parody of Richard Nixon had to go. They insisted the sketch was improper, that it insulted the president. Of course, the magazine itself insulted Nixon in every issue, including a famous pull-out cover that showed Nixon with a Pinocchio-like nose. When RCA made its demands, O'Donoghue rushed into my office and told me about it. "Forget it," I said. "We're not taking anything out." We reached an agreement with RCA and cancelled the contract. Jerry Taylor immediately made a deal with a company called Blue Thumb, run by Bob Krasnow, and *Radio Dinner* eventually came to be, without censorship and with Nixon.

O'Donoghue and Hendra were a strange pairing. O'Donoghue had written some of the most brilliant material in the *Lampoon*: His "Children's Letters to the Gestapo," "Vietnamese Baby Book," and other pieces had marked him as perhaps the most brilliant and scathing satirist of his day, possibly even eclipsing Doug Kenney (who would wind up being an essential part of the scriptwriting team behind *Animal House*). His work usually dealt more with life, growing up, being in school, and relationships, but O'Donoghue attacked the absurdity of the world, doing so with a viciousness and humor that had never been seen before. One day when Michael was in my office, my assistant came in and told him his father was on the phone and it was important. Michael picked up the phone and I could hear his father's voice. "Michael, I have terrible news for you. Your mother lost her toe." Michael immediately snapped back, "Did you look behind the refrigerator?" Bill Murray described O'Donoghue this way: "He hated the horrible things in life and the horrible people in life, and he hated them so well."

It was with *Radio Dinner* that O'Donoghue first introduced the sketch humor that would later light up the *National Lampoon's Radio Hour* and eventually *Saturday Night Live*.

Radio Dinner was a work of genius and it brought the *National Lampoon* into the entertainment business. It was the biggest-selling comedy album of 1972 and was nominated for a Grammy. My reaction was: "Let's do another one." O'Donoghue and Hendra came up with the idea of doing *Lemmings*, a parody of Woodstock. But things happened, as they were wont to do at the *Lampoon*, and O'Donoghue and Hendra were never to speak to each other again.

I still wanted to do the *Lemmings* album but Michael refused and I didn't want to do it without him. The project sat on the shelf. Finally, I suggested to Hendra that a parody of Woodstock would make an interesting musical—why couldn't it be the first *Lampoon* musical comedy? Hendra liked the idea and began work on a script with the actors and other editors of the magazine. O'Donoghue, meanwhile, began work on the *National Lampoon Encyclopedia of Humor* with P.J. O'Rourke.

The first actor to be hired for the new musical was Christopher Guest, who had been exceptionally good on *Radio Dinner*. We also had talks with Melissa Manchester's husband, who managed her career. She too had appeared on *Radio Dinner*, but he thought she was about to move on to much bigger things and she decided to pass.

The first act would be a group of sketches and the second, the Woodstock parody. For that parody we needed actors who could do comedy, sing, and play music. Chris Guest had already made a strong debut on Broadway and was an exceptional musician. He brought with him someone who had been a classmate at Bard College, a piano player who had done very little acting, Chevy Chase. The cast would also include veteran actor Garry Goodrow, Mary-Jennifer Mitchell in the role we had wanted Melissa Manchester for, and Alice Playten, who had made a big splash on TV with a very funny commercial for Alka-Seltzer and was the strongest singer in the cast. Hendra, Guest, and other cast members and *Lampoon* staff would write most of the music along with musical director Paul Jacobs. Jacobs, who orchestrated much of the music for the show, was the classical musician of the group. He had been a child prodigy and given concerts all over the country. He was also a terrific singer and had the perfect rock star look with long flowing red hair and a body that could move in several directions at the same time.

We were missing a centerpiece actor, someone who would MC "Woodshuck," much like Wavy Gravy did at Woodstock, and portray different characters, as well as play sketch comedy in the first act. We had heard that there was some strong talent at Second City in Chicago, so Hendra went out to scout them. He called me the day after his arrival to alert me that there was one guy there who everybody was talking about, a young man named John Belushi. "Can he play music?" I asked. "He said he could," he explained, "and I went with him to a friend's apartment and he picked up a guitar and played a song for me. I asked him if he could play another and he played the same song." Belushi did play drums reasonably well and he did everything else sensationally, so we brought him to New York.

I felt, having seen rehearsals, that we were going to have a hit. Two days before the show opened, Belushi walked into my office looking very sad. "I gotta leave New York," he told me. Incredulously I asked why. "Judy's not happy here," he said. He explained that Judy was his girlfriend and that she had nothing to do all day while he rehearsed and worked on the play and she was lonely and bored. I asked him what Judy did: Did she have a hobby or a special talent? He said she had been an art major at school. I told him that Judy was now a member of the *Lampoon* art department. He smiled. A few days later I learned that this was exactly what John had planned when he came to my office that day. Judy Jacklin later became John's wife.

Lemmings opened at the Village Gate Theater in New York City on January 25, 1973, and it was an immediate success.

This drove O'Donoghue to distraction. Here was an idea that he had helped birth and it was now getting rave reviews and big audiences. Worst of all it was directed by Hendra, a man he could no longer tolerate. He became even angrier and more difficult. He ripped his phone out of the wall socket and broke furniture regularly. One day I walked into his office and his phone was now a skeleton, with the outside casing having been sheared off. Michael stopped talking to Henry Beard because Beard had dated a girl that he had once dated. At one point I was the only one he was talking to. I had to do something. We came up with the *National Lampoon Radio Hour* and I put Michael in charge. Over a two-year period it would be heard on more than 600 stations throughout the country, the most widely listened-to radio program of its time.

After a year or so Michael stopped writing for the magazine. I remember walking down Second Avenue with him after dinner telling him that I wanted him to start writing again, in addition to producing the *Radio Hour*. He agreed. Only a week or so later, on Super Bowl Sunday, he called me at home while I was watching the game. He told me that Anne Beatts, then his girlfriend, had to have a desk in the *Radio Hour* office. I was annoyed that he would call me at that hour with such a request and told him to talk to me about it the next day at work. He got even angrier than usual and said that if I didn't resolve this issue at that moment he would leave. I was tired of the threats and the battles and I told him he could, indeed, leave if he chose to. I list this as very high on the list of stupidest moments in my life.

Lemmings ran for two years, went on to have a road company, and a few months after it closed, we started working on another revue, *The National Lampoon Show*, which Belushi starred in and directed. The cast of that show included Gilda Radner, Harold Ramis, Bill Murray, his brother Brian Doyle-Murray, Joe Flaherty, and others. A second company included Meat Loaf, Ellen Foley, Mimi Kennedy, and Richard Belzer.

After touring the country, I decided to bring the show to New York for a limited engagement, long enough for reviews and features. I'd met a young Canadian producer, Ivan Reitman, who agreed to come to New York and supervise the show.

Harold Ramis remembers the first rehearsal for the New York opening. It was a cold, snowy day. Everybody came in wearing winter clothing. The cast had started rehearsing when Ivan walked in. It was his first day with the show. He had on a woolen stocking hat, a big scarf, and a heavy jacket. He was grinning broadly as he greeted everybody. As he did, he took off the hat and scarf and jacket. When he was finished, Bill

Murray put an arm around his shoulder and, picking up the clothing Ivan had discarded, put them back on him piece by piece. Then—and Ivan was still grinning—he walked him to the door, opened it, eased him out, and slammed the door shut. Ivan didn't return for two days. And when he did, he never mentioned what had happened.

6

WE'RE GONNA MAKE A MOVIE!

In late 1974 Marvin Antonowsky of NBC came to my office and asked if I would be interested in doing a *National Lampoon* weekly variety show for television. I thought about it for over a week. I had three kids growing up. I ran a busy and successful company. It would have been too much. A weekly comedy television revue would be an exhausting full-time job, as Lorne Michaels would later prove. It was something one had to dedicate their life to. I passed on the offer.

A few months later NBC put together a show that included mostly *Lampoon* graduates and a format very much like the *Lampoon Radio Hour*; this, of course, was *Saturday Night Live*.

By 1975 the *National Lampoon* had reached new heights in publishing, record albums, special editions, a radio show, and now two revues that toured America. It was also the year that a five-year option, installed when a deal with Beard, Kenney, and Hoffman was first struck, would kick in. As part of that deal, we had given them, after five years, the option to have their share of the company bought out. Because the company was showing strong profits, the price was now $7.5 million. I turned to our investment brokers, knowing that the country was in a recession and the market had dropped dismally. As I expected, there could be no underwriting to raise the money. We had part of it in the bank but needed additional funding to close the deal. I called Steve Ross at Warners, he loaned us the money, and we made the purchase.

Beard immediately retired, announcing to the staff that this was "the happiest day of his life;" Kenney parceled off part of what he got to O'Donoghue and others who had worked with him and agreed to stay on as a staff writer or writer. A year later he came to me and told me he had to leave. He was exhausted, tired from nearly six years of deadlines. Once again I was faced with losing a key player. I knew he loved show business and without really thinking I snapped, "You can't leave now! We're gonna make a movie!"

Doug's second reaction, after first being delighted with the idea, was to ask if I had any thoughts about what the movie was going to be. I had none.

We toyed with it for a week or so. We thought about building a screenplay around his growing up in Ohio. No. Then, perhaps, life at the *Harvard Lampoon*. No. Harvard is too elite. He suggested *Teenage Commies from Outer Space*, the book he had written during one of his disappearances, or perhaps a full-length version of his short story "My First Blowjob." I could see that one on the marquee of a movie theater in Des Moines. No! No! No! We finally decided it would be based on the

1964 *High School Yearbook*, the popular parody of everybody's yearbook that Doug had edited with P.J. O'Rourke, after originally creating it as a short piece in the magazine.

Meanwhile, without our knowing it, Ivan Reitman and Harold Ramis had started discussing the possibility of doing a movie on their own.

Ramis says that Reitman first spoke to Belushi, Bill Murray, and Brian Doyle-Murray and asked them to start writing a film comedy. He said he'd pay the three of them $2,500. They wanted $2,500 each. Reitman told them, "I can get Ramis for 2,500 dollars," and he did.

When it became known that we were, the four of us, working on film projects, Ivan and I decided to do it together, as a *Lampoon* movie.

So, Ramis and Kenney started making notes and came up with a high school movie in which Charles Manson was a student and he and the other students were doing drugs, getting laid, and having drunken orgies.

"No," I said. "These are teenagers. We can't do these things in high school."

So we moved it to college.

The writers started kicking ideas around. Doug may have gone to an Ivy League university, but the parties were the same in nearly all other colleges, only the booze and pot were more expensive.

But we just weren't happy with what they came up with. Doug suggested we bring in Chris Miller, who was the *Lampoon* short story guru. Many of his stories were based on his frat life at Dartmouth. Why not include him in the mix and build the movie around the same kind of crazy fraternity that Chris had belonged to and was now writing about, the one called Delta House.

When we asked Chris to join the team, he just nodded and smiled broadly. He reminded them that his frat at Dartmouth was known on campus as "the Animal House." Everybody agreed that that would be the title of the screenplay they were to write.

The three men all came from different places when they joined together to write the screenplay. Doug grew up in a middle-class family from Chagrin Falls, Ohio. His father was a tennis pro, and Doug grew up as an excellent tennis player. But at Harvard he lettered in partying and the *Harvard Lampoon*.

One would never know what Doug's next move would be. In 1973, Len Mogel was teaching at New York University and invited Doug to give a lecture in his class. Doug walked in, looked at Mogel and the students in the audience, then slid open the door to a closet and proceeded to give his lecture from inside the closed closet. About halfway through, he came out and continued while sitting cross-legged on Mogel's desk.

Soon after that, I decided to send Kenney on a college speaking tour around the country. I first asked him to, please, do all his speeches in front of a microphone and not from inside a closet. He did three or four speeches, usually referencing his stories or his own days at Harvard. The reports I got back often included the word "meandering" when commenting on his speeches. Doug and I agreed that this clearly wasn't one of his finer attributes and instead I asked Chris to finish the tour. He would do readings of the short stories he wrote in the *Lampoon*. That worked fine, until one day he read the wrong story in the wrong place.

"It was South Missouri State Teacher's College," Chris remembers, "and I went there and they had me doing a lunchtime performance in their cafeteria. Little did they know what they were getting into 'cause I started reading 'Pinto's First Lay' and it opens with a guy talking about corn-holing his girlfriend. When I hit that part, silence spread throughout the cafeteria. This one woman jumped to her feet and ran out. It turned out that she was the one who had hired me; she went to her boyfriend, who was some kind of a big wheel there at the college and he came to the cafeteria, walked up to me, and stopped. I looked up and smiled. 'Yes?' And he didn't meet my eyes. He just grabbed my microphone and turned it off and said, 'This show is now over.' So he left and nobody knew what to do next—it was a weird situation. The kids there said they wanted to hear the rest of the story, so we went out to the lawn, I stood beneath a tree and finished reading the story. And the kids were gathered around me and by the time I was done and ready to leave there were reporters there from the local TV station."

That reaction was one of the kind of happenings that *Animal House* was born from.

Harold tells of Doug going to his apartment to work on the script one day. Harold was changing clothes and Doug walked over to a bookcase, pulled out a book he had never seen before, looked at the title, and when Harold returned to the room, he proceeded to unravel an entirely new story based solely on the title of the book and a few of the characters from the first couple of pages. It was a different story than the printed version but he went chapter by chapter with his new tale, and according to Harold, "wrote" a much better book in ten minutes. Harold looked at him in amazement. Doug shrugged and said, "I can do that with any book."

As for Harold, he came from Chicago and went to George Washington University in St. Louis and, like Doug, got high marks in partying. While at Washington, Ramis remembered hitting golf balls at some ROTC troops who were training on a nearby green. This was one of the first scenes put into the movie treatment and, again, that was precisely the kind of comedy we wanted.

Soon after graduating college, he joined Second City in Chicago and then on to the *National Lampoon Radio Hour*, the *National Lampoon Show*, and *SCTV* in Toronto. In all these venues he would be both an actor and writer, and like Beard, he was always one whose cohorts would go to for advice. On the road with the *National Lampoon Show*, he solved problems.

One such problem involved Gilda Radner, who was deathly afraid of flying. On the road with the revue, it was always pre-arranged that the troop would travel by car or bus, or by train for longer distances. On one occasion, the distance was too great and the time too short. The company manager announced that everyone had to fly. Gilda refused. Harold said that he'd convince her she should do it. They spent the entire night together, Ramis plying her with assorted drugs and pep talks, the basic theme of which was "the show must go on." The next morning, the cast gathered in the hotel lobby to board the bus taking them to the airport. Everyone kept glancing at their watches as departure time approached, but there was no Gilda. Finally, the elevator door opened, and Gilda, one arm entwined with Harold's, eyes glazed, and body moving only barely, emerged. Around her neck was hung a handwritten sign that read HI! I'M GILDA AND I'M NOT AFRAID TO FLY! She wore it until the plane landed and they got her to the next hotel.

After his years at Dartmouth, Chris Miller had gone on to work for a Madison Avenue ad agency. I asked him why he left advertising and what happened after that.

"I was working for an agency called Dancer Fitzgerald Sample. I was more and more feeling like I had to get out of there because I wanted to grow my hair long and be a hippie and I couldn't do that while I was ensconced in an office on Madison Avenue. One day I was having lunch with some 'suits' and they were having drinks with their lunch, in time-honored Madison Avenue fashion. I had some pot in a baggy in my pocket and I put some in my soup, because you have to heat marijuana to have it be effective, and next thing I knew, I was fired.

"Soon after I heard from Doug Kenney saying he wanted to meet me, so we met. A guy named David Standish who was at *Playboy* had told him about me and I had submitted stuff to the *Lampoon* before, but as you know nobody read stuff that was submitted cold from the outside. Because Standish called him, Doug read it and thought it was pretty good so he hired me to write short stories and some of them were about my days at Dartmouth."

Since Chris's days at his Dartmouth fraternity were used as the basis for the plot it was easy to come up with the names for the Deltas. As a matter of fact, they had a real Otter and a real Flounder and a lot of other colorful names that were not used. They had an Eel and a Troll. There was a Bluto but he wasn't in Chris's frat. Their version of Bluto was named Hydrant: You can figure out his body shape just from the name. Chris tells of when he was at Dartmouth: "We used to burn our bush, set our pubic hairs on fire, which makes a loud crackling sound. We used to raid this one fraternity, but we never did anything to the dean. No horses—we never killed a horse."

Flounder, in the original Delta House, was not the Flounder we knew and loved in *Animal House*. He was dry, witty, and savage. He feared nothing and certainly had no fear of saying anything. In Miller's book *The Real Animal House*, one story goes as follows:

> Flounder majored in dissipation. It is said that once, on some big weekend, a girl came up, put a hand on his shoulder, and said, "How are you, Flounder?" In his Charles Laughton voice, he replied, "If you would remove your hand from my shoulder and place it upon my genitals, all would be well."

History does not record the young lady's response.

And there was an Otter too. In the magazine *Ampersand*, reporter Susan Pile wrote about that and the female reaction to Tim Matheson's character. It adds to the amazement at Tim's never having reached stardom.

Every girl I know who saw *Animal House* wished she had been laid by the inimitable Otter. This is probably because no one I know ever encountered such a master of the art of seduction on any college campus in America. "Mr. Thoughtful with a dozen roses for y-o-u," cooed Otter, as he stepped blithely into the room at the one-shot motel where the neo-Nazis of the Omega House were waiting to give him his comeuppance.

It's hard to believe a character like Otter ever existed, but he most definitely did. Chris Miller, one of the three writers of *Animal House*, knew a guy called—you got it—Otter, back at Dartmouth in the sixties and wrote him into the script as the rush chairman of the Deltas. Finding someone to play the part in the movie was another story. Where is the young Cary Grant now that we need him, to uplift the spirit and deface the moral fiber of the women of America?

Not only the tone but the origination of the infamous "double secret probation" came from his school days. It seems that, once again, Chris's original Delta House was in trouble with the authorities. In the book, Delta Truck warns the frats:

> "All right. Listen up. Now that the buck stops at me, here's what I have to say. We've got a triple warning, right? Only one in the college's history. We have to be extremely careful—if the administration catches one bad hair coming out of our noses, we're on pro."

"If we fart within five miles of Parkhurst Hall," shouted Hydrant, "we're on pro."

"If we say fuck on campus over one decibel, we're on pro," said Black Whit.

"All right, shut up, you assholes. Just remember, if we do go on pro, there'll be no beer, no girls, no nothing. All the house'll be good for is sleeping in. So stay in touch with your higher brain functions and don't fuck things up for your brothers, okay?" Dumptruck regarded them seriously.

No one spoke. A sobering admonition indeed.

Truck smiled benevolently. "And now, let us drink."

The writers met regularly in their homes, my home, and often in the boardroom of the *Lampoon*. I would sit in on those meetings as would Ivan, who flew in from Toronto several times. On one occasion the three of them flew to Toronto to spend some time with him. The treatment was moving along and the pages I read every day were wonderfully funny, but they still bothered me. During our meetings in the boardroom, I kept yelling, "Black hats! White hats!" I felt that the reader, and thus the film audience, didn't, and wouldn't, like the Deltas as much as they should. The audience needed to be rooting for them. It had to be clear who the good guys were and who the bad guys were, and it seemed to me that it wasn't. We changed things, cut things, and trimmed things.

The only one of the five of us who had made a movie before was Ivan, who had produced what I call triple-z films in Canada: very low-budget movies, including *Cannibal Girls, The Columbus of Sex,* and *They Came from Within.* At least one of those films featured someone with three arms. Making an independent movie, the way Ivan had in Canada, wasn't exactly the road I wanted to take. My plan was that we'd write a movie and sell it to Hollywood—and I knew where I was going to take it.

So Doug, Harold, and Chris wrote a treatment. A treatment is normally twenty to thirty pages long. Ours was 114 pages long. I remember one studio executive later saying, "This is like *War and Peace* on speed. Usually I read a treatment in fifteen to twenty minutes, this one took two hours." The ideas were there, as was the humor, but it was all over the place and I had great doubts about some of the elements in it.

And so we kept at it. We had a treatment that had taken nearly a year to write and wasn't exactly structured, but we were sure we had something.

While the treatment was being written, Doug and Chris were back writing for the *Lampoon* and Harold was writing for television in the states, eventually becoming the head writer and one of the stars of *SCTV.* The movie was, for the moment, on hold. But it would soon go on to consume all our lives.

7

THE TOUGH SELL

Right from the start it was decided that the lead character would be named Larry Kroger, after the principal character in the *High School Yearbook*. He was a Doug Kenney creation. Doug also took the name Mandy Pepperidge from the *High School Yearbook*. Mandy was one of the four leading ladies in *Animal House*. Chris Miller decided that Larry Kroger's Delta name would be Pinto, which was the name he had when he belonged to the Deltas at Dartmouth. It seems that he had spilled some hot tar on his penis when he was a boy and a mark remained, thus "Pinto," since the breed of horse of the same name has patches of white and black on his skin.

John Belushi was always going to be Bluto; the heavyset body, the grizzly beard, made him a perfect Bluto, as in the Popeye cartoons. Dean Wormer was taken in part from President Nixon, with a touch or two of Miller's dean at Dartmouth.

Finally in mid-1976, with these characters and a story

taking shape, we had a viable treatment. The film was set in the early sixties and reflected the party life of college fraternities during that time. It was a great period for wild times, and wild times was what this treatment was all about.

As planned, I turned first to Steve Ross at Warners. He reacted positively at once when I told him I had the treatment for the first *Lampoon* movie. Ten minutes later, Jay Emmett, the president of Warners, called. "I'm leaving for LA tomorrow," he said. "Send me the treatment and I'll bring it to Ted Ashley (the head of then subsidiary Warner Bros.). He'll read it immediately." I wasn't so sure that was the way to go. I asked him if I could meet with Ashley first, talk to him about the treatment, and then let him read it. My thinking was that a studio head might not really understand the *National Lampoon* and its humor, and *Animal House* was pure *Lampoon* humor. Jay persisted: "Ashley reports to me and Steve and we want to make a *Lampoon* movie." So I sent the treatment over to him.

Three days later Steve phoned me. "Jay just called from LA. Ashley read the treatment last night and said it would never make a movie. Jay wanted him to reread it but Ashley was adamant about it. I'm his boss, Matty, but Ted's the movie expert and I don't want to go over his head."

Going over his head was the move I had planned right from the start. Go to Steve or Jay and have them bring it to Warner Bros. It didn't work. Now I had to figure out what to do next. I didn't know anyone else in the film business. Ivan knew only Canadian investors and suggested we go that route. He could raise money in Canada and we could make a low-budget movie, but there was no way I would agree to that. The

Lampoon was succeeding at everything we did. We had to do this right. No $80,000 budget. No Canadian distributor. We go big or we don't go at all.

Now came the strange stroke of luck that nearly every great project seems to need, particularly in the movie business. The legendary Sam Goldwyn once said, "Success in making moves is 30 percent talent, 30 percent connections, and 80 percent luck." His math was famously incorrect but his philosophy wasn't. Out of the blue, I got a call from one Jerry Miller. He identified himself as Ned Tanen's assistant, Tanen being the president of Universal Studios. "Mr. Simmons," he said, "I've been a *Lampoon* fan since the first issue. If you ever decide to make a movie, we'd be very interested." He couldn't see my smile, as we spoke.

"It just so happens," I said slowly, "that I might have a film treatment."

He was excited. "I'll come by and pick it up."

"No," I said. "If the studio is interested, I'll fly to LA and meet with Mr. Tanen. I want to talk to him about this first and then he can read it."

Two days later I got a call from Miller. "Mr. Tanen will meet you anytime." Tanen was a career Universal executive. He'd actually started in the mailroom there and was now the third-largest stockholder in MCA, then the parent company of Universal. The two biggest stockholders were the company's founder, Jules Stein, who had by now retired, and Lew Wasserman, once Stein's right-hand man.

Ivan and I flew to LA only a week after Miller's call. We checked in to the Beverly Hills Hotel and met with Tanen the next day. I told him the story and he quietly nodded. He was a true studio executive. His face looked like it had been chiseled out of granite and you had the feeling the chair he sat in was up higher than those we were sitting on. Ivan sat quietly, chiming in with a word or two about the treatment. Tanen agreed to read it that night.

The next day Jerry Miller called and asked us to come back to the studio that afternoon. Tanen greeted us: "I hate this treatment! Everybody is drunk, or high, or getting laid. I'd never make this movie—except you're the *National Lampoon*." He looked at me with that granite face, "Can you make this movie for three million?" I didn't have the slightest idea what the budget for the film would be. I looked at Ivan. His answer was an empty shrug.

I turned back to Tanen, "Absolutely," I said. "I guarantee it." He agreed to develop the screenplay.

I flew back to New York and Ivan to Toronto. The writers were ecstatic when they heard the news. Kenney, the film buff, had wanted to make a movie more than anything else. Ramis, now being seen on *SCTV*, felt a movie at Universal would be the big time and Miller, of course, had long believed his short stories could transfer to film.

The rest of the staff wasn't quite as ecstatic. Before he'd left in 1975, Beard had said he never wanted us to go into the entertainment business. He always felt the magazine would suffer if we did. He was probably right. Once *Animal House* happened, many of the writers moved to film and television where the money was infinitely better. In addition to staffers and contributors leaving, some of the *Harvard Lampoon* people went directly to television, instead of stopping off and working at the *National Lampoon*, as had been the case during the first decade of the magazine.

Beard had been a literary person. He believed in the tradition of *The New Yorker* and of the *Harvard Lampoon*, and he wanted to see the *Lampoon* humor stay in print. Others, like Hendra, were unhappy that they weren't included in the mix. And P.J. O'Rourke stated very clearly that he had no desire to make movies and, as a matter of fact, with one brief exception, to this day he has never been involved with moviemaking, despite his popularity. Like Beard, he was a man of letters, and he has remained that way.

I flew back to LA a week later, this time accompanied by the *Lampoon*'s entertainment attorney, Bob Levine. Bob had never negotiated a movie contract before. I, of course, had never even seen one. I was warned before I left, "Don't trust these people! They'll steal you blind! And don't take net points." Net points are percentages of the profit of a movie. In more recent years, after stars and major directors would only make a movie in which they received a share of the gross, net points have become even less valuable. Eddie Murphy, a few years ago, characterized them as "monkey points" because before reaching net, the studios include their overhead and various other expenses, even a percentage tacked on top of a movie's paid advertising. Rarely is there anything left for the net participants.

When we sat down in the office of Universal's head of business affairs, Mel Sattler, the first thing I said was "No net points!" Sattler complained for a while, explaining that almost nobody, except for a few major stars, were getting gross points.

In 1976 that was true, but I shook my head and held my ground. "Okay," he relented. "I'll give you five percent of the gross from breakeven." Again, I shook my head. "Ten percent from breakeven." Again, he complained, then after a while, agreed. I jumped right in: "And fifteen percent of all gross receipts over 15 million." He looked at me like I was crazy and we heard another lecture on current profit-sharing policy, but again he finally agreed. When he did, I snapped, "And I want twenty percent of everything over 20 million." He adamantly refused to go there. I shrugged and we stared at each other for a while, then argued some more. It was finally agreed that we would get 17.5 percent of everything over $20 million.

Two hours later we'd hammered out a deal. They agreed to all the demands I had made on percentages of gross profits. I had what I wanted, a rising share of gross profits that would mean important income if the movie was a hit. And I felt certain it would be.

To my knowledge, this was the best profit participation deal anyone at that time had gotten from a major studio. I believe that Universal thought this little movie might gross $8 million or $10 million at the box office and that the contract they agreed to was only an exercise in deal making.

We would be happy to prove them wrong.

8

THEY LOVE IT! THEY HATE IT!

In Dennis McDougal's book *The Last Mogul*, about Universal uber-boss Lew Wasserman, he talks about having problems with the hiring of a first time producer: *"National Lampoon publisher Matty Simmons, who brought the idea [of Animal House] to Universal, had never made a movie before in his life but Tanen let Simmons produce, over Wasserman's misgivings."*

An agent representing the writers wrapped up their deal a few days later, and they started to write the screenplay. When I returned to LA occasionally to meet with studio executives, Jerry Miller, the assistant who had first contacted me, was suddenly gone. No one knew exactly where he'd gone and I've never seen or heard of him since; but he remains the man who "found" *Animal House*.

At the time, Thom Mount was a young vice president at Universal and Sean Daniel, who had been a political activist in New York, was a junior executive. For weeks after seeing the treatment they read it and reread it and tried to figure out how they could get something past the brass—Tanen basically being the brass. Daniel remembers thinking that he and Mount thought the treatment was incredibly funny, and that there was a script in there somewhere. But it wasn't there yet. It had beer kegs flying through a Kennedy float in a parade and hitting JFK's head in the same area the actual bullet had. They shuddered.

"The exit wound," Daniel still remembers. "That was just one thing. The treatment had every outrageous thing you guys could think of. It also had tremendous heart. The characters were great. They were multidimensional and people could relate to them. But Tanen and the others at the studio couldn't relate to it. Tanen would say to Thom and me, 'Look, what is this? I mean, what the hell is this? This guy sleeps with the young kid's girlfriend and tries to sleep with every other girl on campus. The other guy is a Peeping Tom. And they're like downtown drunks, and they're the heroes?!' But Tanen knew there was something there and he didn't want to put it into turnaround. He felt [we] were on to something and I remember one day in his office telling him, 'We have something hilarious here that we should make. This guy Belushi is gonna become an amazing star. And the other characters are wonderful.' And I remember telling him that [we] knew that there were elements of the picture that had to be cut."

He shrugged as he recalled, "I was the only one at the studio who had seen *Lemmings*. And had seen what Belushi could do and what *Lampoon* humor could be. Thom and I were also probably the only ones who had read the magazine regularly, and we loved it! We tried to make [the studio] realize we were sitting on something that would speak to young people, in the way the magazine had, and the radio show, the comedy albums, and *Saturday Night Live*, now only a year or so old, were doing."

But the people around Mount and Daniel were shocked by the script. They had never done anything like it, and they didn't *like* it. Mostly, they were afraid to put their corporate name on it, and would say, "This is beneath us." Or "We don't do this sort of thing."

But Tanen continued to be reluctant to pass on it and kept demanding scripts and new scripts and rewrites of scripts. Daniel didn't think the execs at Universal had read the script, but Ned and his team were concerned about what they would think about making such a movie.

"Ned was always kind of at war with them," Sean recalls. "So there was almost a part of him who continued [work on] the movie just to be contrary. Just to shock them. Even though he kept complaining about the rewrites. And once when I raved about one of the newer drafts, he told me to get the hell out of his office."

"Everybody ridiculed me for being so rough on *Animal House*," Tanen would later say. "But remember, I'm the one who green-lighted it."

According to Daniel, Tanen was the only one there, at that time, who could green-light a movie. MCA president Sidney Sheinberg and Wasserman kept out of that part of the business, as that was their deal with Tanen. And with that deal came recriminations if the film he green-lighted was a flop.

The day after I read the latest script, I sat in the office with the pages on my desk in front of me. Doug strolled in, looked at the script. I just nodded. He smiled and left.

Chris has told me that the three of them wrote the script on what he called "marijuana production." All three were longtime marijuana devotees and seemed to do their best work with a joint in one hand and the other hand on the typewriter keys.

Their method of collaboration involved the occasional get-together, but they also worked on their own, each taking a section, coming up with a rough draft, and then turning it over to the others, so the scenes involved would go back and forth, until everyone had a whack at it and everybody was satisfied with it.

Chris told me that he always felt that both Harold and Doug were geniuses. To this day, he says that working with them was the most fun he has ever had in his life.

And now after a year of writing and rewriting 1,000 notes and having 1,000 arguments, we had a script. There would be more changes to come, particularly after the director was hired, but we knew that in the 152 pages there was a solid 110 that was a good script.

And it went something like this:

The setting is Faber College, in the fictional town of Faber. First, we meet the good guys and the bad. The "good" guys are the Omegas, smart, sophisticated, and in charge. And we hate them immediately.

Then there are the "bad" guys, the Deltas: sloppy, uncivilized, and majoring full-time in boozing, sex, and the challenge of spending their lives in college without learning anything. We love them at once and endure their pranks, their lack of respect for anything that resembles the law, and their truly devious search for good times.

We meet the freshmen, Larry Kroger, to be nicknamed Pinto, and Kent Dorfman, tagged with the name Flounder.

Then there's D-Day, who slips in and out of the film like a mysterious shadow, always on hand for a party but never a class.

There's Hoover, the frat president who begs for order but not too reluctantly accepts chaos.

There's Otter: scoundrel, womanizer, and leader.

Boone, lover of jazz, beer, and his girl Katy—not neessarily in that order.

But, most of all, there's John Blutarsky, Bluto, an anarchistic devil, who when facing expulsion moans, "Seven years of college down the drain." He is an everyman hero and is, indeed, the film's antihero.

Then there is Dean Wormer, who spits villainy and, with the Omegas, is on a lifetime crusade to destroy the Deltas.

We go through frat initiatons, toga parties that feature a bedsheet-clad group of misfits dancing to "Shout!," a food fight in the school cafeteria, and a pickup scene so brilliant that it is, by far, the king of all pickup scenes. A highlight is the sequence in a black bar in which the Deltas lose their dates and exit in a panic with Flounder screaming his classic, albeit politically incorrect "The Negroes stole our dates!"

We meet the kind of professor we all wanted to have in school. He teaches them poetry, teaches Pinto about the wonders of pot, and winds up sleeping with Boone's girl.

The Deltas have their share of good times, but with grade averages ranging from 0.0 to 1.2, their fraternity gets booted out of school. The only answer, they decide, is to wreck the school's Homecoming Parade, an action scene filled with so many comedic moments, it was practically a movie in itself.

Along the way, there would be a fraternity courtroom scene in which the Deltas are tried for their misdeeds and wind up marching out in song, with Dean Wormer screaming, "There'll be no more fun of any kind!" There would be Pinto's first lay, and the night Bluto, Flounder, and D-Day kill a horse (accidentally, of course).

There would be all this and more. The overarching moral of the screenplay was: There's a lot of "bad" in some of us and a little "bad" in all of us.

After approving the final script the studio budgeted the picture and told us to make it for $2.8 million. We had to shoot it in thirty-two days. And, of course, we still needed a director.

9

DOES ANYBODY WANT TO DIRECT
THIS THING?

It was now early 1977 and we started searching for a director. There'd be no green light until we had a completed script and a director that Tanen approved of. In New York, our screenwriters were working daily and the first draft of the script was nearly completed.

The studio approached Bob Rafelson who had so brilliantly directed *Five Easy Pieces*, as well as seven other directors with strong credits. They all passed. I met with Bob Clark, the director whose film *A Christmas Story* remains, to this day, one of the most popular holiday movies. Clark read the early pages of the treatment and he too passed. He felt it was too "rowdy" for him. (After *Animal House*'s huge success, Clark directed *Porky's*, a far more "rowdy" film.) He, like many others, wasn't quite ready for *Animal House*. Sean Daniel would lead us to just the right choice.

One day, while I was at Universal, Daniel told me that his girlfriend at the time had been the script supervisor on a little film called *Kentucky Fried Movie*, directed by a new-comer named John Landis. The picture was being screened in a preview that night and I agreed to go with Sean to see it. After watching it, I was enthused. "I think," I told Daniel, "that this guy has our sensibilities. By that I mean that he probably has no respect for authority, very low morals, and continually roots for the underdog."

Daniel smiled. "I thought you'd like it. And I gave Landis a copy of the script and he wants to do it."

"I want to meet with him," I said. "Should we ask Tanen first?"

Daniel told me I should call Tanen, which surprised me and I asked him why *he* wouldn't ask him since Tanen was his boss. "Well," he said, "I think we should all push for this." I had a feeling he didn't want to once again confront Tanen, who hadn't seen *Kentucky Fried Movie* but might have thought differently of it than we did.

The next day I called Tanen and had the strangest conversation with him.

"Ned? Matty."

"Yeah, Matty."

"I think we've got the right guy to direct this movie. John Landis."

"You like him?"

"Yes."

"Okay, bye, Matty."

That was our conversation.

So Ned, according to Daniel and Mount, was saying,

"All right, you guys have worked me over and you've gotten the script down. Now go make it and make it funny!"

"His tone," Daniel recalls, "was threatening. We thought, what happens to us if it doesn't come out funny?"

We knew we were going in the right direction with the script but it still need more work. We didn't quite know what we were getting with Landis. *Kentucky Fried Movie* was funny and it had "our" sensibilities but it was undisciplined. Now we were making a major studio movie. Despite being somewhat apprehensive, we felt he just might be the perfect director for *Animal House.*

Now that we had Ned's approval, I invited Landis to visit me at Universal. Actually, we were across the street from Universal. The studio thought so little of the film, they had parked Ivan and me at a motel across from the lot. Motel rooms had been transformed into offices with cheap furniture and one secretary whom we shared.

Landis walked into my office. He looked at me very humbly. "Mr. Simmons," he greeted me. "It would be the greatest thrill of my life if you hired me to direct the first *National Lampoon* film." (To this day, I tease John by saying that that was the last humble thing he's ever said.)

As we sat and talked, Landis's personality changed. He became the Landis we now know, eager to talk and tell you stories, to exchange ideas, always with a flare. Certainly, he is one of the most colorful people in the industry. That flare, that color, and the excitement in the room that day, shows on the screen when he directs a film.

I later learned from him the story of *Kentucky Fried Movie*, the film that had impressed us: "The most amazing thing to me," he said, "is that *Kentucky Fried Movie* hadn't come out when I was offered the [*Animal House*] job. *Kentucky Fried* cost around $540,000. We shot ten minutes of it in order to raise the money and that cost about $38,000. The producer, Bob Weiss, and I worked for free and the Zucker brothers put up the money; we shot it and then got the rest of the money and made the movie. It grossed $48 million but the secret was that it was financed by the guy who owned the United Artists theater circuit, and I think one of the reasons it made so much money, honestly, is because whenever a picture wasn't performing, he would pull it and stick *Kentucky Fried Movie* in one of his theaters. *Kentucky Fried* was released while we were shooting [*Animal House*] because I remember a bunch of the cast went to see it and they came back like, 'Uh-oh.'"

After he was hired, John Landis flew to New York to meet the three writers. Their coolness to him was obvious. They figured he was some Hollywood guy and they weren't high on Hollywood guys, plus they didn't want to be told what was funny and what wasn't. To this day, he describes that meeting as "hostile." They soon changed their ways. After the studio green-lighted the script he told the writers that he didn't have the budget for it but if they flew to the location, he would hire them as actors and they'd work every day.

Harold passed. He was unhappy that he didn't get the role of Boone himself, and he and his wife went to Greece, where he stayed for several months. But Doug and Chris took John up on the offer. They not only played their roles perfectly as Delta House members Stork and Hardbar, but they made numerous suggestions. Landis remembers, "During the toga party, when the dancers suddenly dropped to the ground to "Shout!" doing what was called in the film "the gator," while that scene was being filmed, Doug suggested that we include that. I thought he was kidding and said, 'Doug, you are so full of shit.' Doug persisted and asked people round the set if they knew what the gator was. Some did. So we put it into the scene."

There was no question of casting John Belushi as the comic lead. But it came time to focus on the rest of the cast. And for an ensemble film with a controversial script and a small budget, the choices to be made in casting could make or break our project.

10

FINDING THE ANIMALS

The difficulty in dealing with the studio had been in the script process. With Landis on board, we could now focus on hiring the right cast. We retained a young casting director named Michael Chinich, whom Thom Mount had worked with before. His casting, particularly of the young Deltas and Omegas, was superior to that of any comedy movie before or after *Animal House*. There has never been anything in comedy equal to the acting strength and perfect casting that came out of our film. And although we all contributed in several ways, it was Chinich who brought in the comparative unknowns for the right roles and helped make the movie what it is.

Tanen wanted comics like Buddy Hackett and Shecky Greene to play roles like Wormer and Mayor DePasto. We disagreed, insisting that good dramatic actors take such roles. He said we had to have some big names in the film and suggested teaming Belushi, who had been set from the start, with Dan Ackroyd, and then perhaps bringing in Chevy Chase. I was opposed to either choice because I wanted this to be a *National Lampoon* movie and not a *Saturday Night Live* movie. Having three *Saturday Night Live* stars in the film certainly would have identified it in that way. Landis felt the same way about Chevy, if for different reasons. John felt that Chevy was too over the top for the role. Otter had to be a kind of stand-back, cool womanizer, where Chevy was always the clown. Chevy was already a celebrity. He was the first star to come out of *SNL* and Landis felt that the Deltas should not be played by stars. They should be identified as Otter, Pinto, Flounder, and so on, and not by their previous starring roles.

Chevy was briefly considered, and though he did like the role of Otter, it was the money and, perhaps more important, the idea of starring in a movie opposite Goldie Hawn—*Foul Play*—that led him to pass on the role of Otter. Landis does remember a lunch with Chevy during which he reminded Chevy that starring opposite Goldie made him like "Cary Grant," and by contrast *Animal House* was just a bunch of guys. (I have known Chevy for many years and I don't think he could have been conned so easily. He obviously had already decided to do *Foul Play*.)

It's unlikely, in any case, that we could have met Chevy's asking price. Belushi was the highest-paid actor in *Animal House*. He got $40,000.

Landis jokes, "Actually the highest-paid actor in the movie was the horse."

•   •   •

The studio still wanted another name or two in the movie. Landis came up with Donald Sutherland. He had met Sutherland on the set of *Kelly's Heroes* in Yugoslavia and they had become friends. However, the studio wanted a star but wouldn't *pay* for a star. So Landis approached Sutherland and asked for a favor. Donald would be shooting *Invasion of the Body Snatchers*, so Landis, in his usual unrealistic way, suggested, "You can do your part for us in one day!" Then Landis was told by the studio that you can't hire an actor for just one day because you have to hire an actor for at least a day plus one, in case he doesn't finish in one day. So Landis pleaded and pleaded and Sutherland finally agreed. Now came the real challenge, making a deal that Sutherland would approve. He first asked for $250,000 and, in Landis's words, "The studio said, 'Get the fuck outta here!'"

Instead, they offered him a mere $20,000 for what would probably be a day, with a day's hold, plus points. Sutherland didn't want points. "I can't take that offer. I just want the money, I don't want any points in the movie."

So now Landis got back in the act and pleaded some more with Sutherland, and he ended up doing it for $35,000, no points, for a day plus one. He even brought his own wig (the same one he had worn in *Don't Look Now*).

Incidentally, if Sutherland had taken the $20,000 and the points, he likely would have cleared at least $6 million.

He's frequently reminded of that and just chuckles.

Landis wanted Jack Webb, best known for his role on *Dragnet*, for the part of Dean Wormer, and had lunch with Webb to discuss it. "Webb sat there drinking Scotch and smoking the whole time, just looking at me like Joe Friday as I pitched the movie. He called the next day after he read the script and said, "John, I appreciate the offer but you're out of your goddamn mind!"

Ivan had been friendly with the wonderful dramatic actor John Vernon and suggested him for the role. Landis was apprehensive but then watched Vernon in the Clint Eastwood film *The Outlaw Josie Wales*. In it, Vernon had a big black beard and steely blue eyes; he could make you shudder when he played the villain. Landis remembers when he was watching the movie: "There was a huge close-up and Vernon had this great line where he said, 'Don't piss down my leg and tell me it's raining.' When I saw and heard his voice, which was like venom, and thought of the line in our script, 'The time has come for someone to put his foot down and that foot is me!' I knew that he was our man."

John Vernon, born Adolphus Raymondus Vernon Agopsowicz in Saskatchewan, was a celebrated television, film, and stage actor in Canada before coming to Hollywood. He spent a year with the Royal Shakespeare Company in Stratford-upon-Avon in England. When John said "Hello" you knew he had done Shakespeare. His voice was rich and vibrant. In American films, he appeared mostly as a villain, in *Dirty Harry, Point Blank, 1984*, and many others. The veteran character actor read a few passages of the script and we knew he was the perfect choice for Dean Wormer. Even his eyes could snarl.

So we went ahead and cast him and when the studio

heard about it, Ned called Landis, Sean, and Thom up to his office at Universal and screamed at them.

"He *roared* at us." Daniel remembers. "'You're hiring fucking TV actors!' This, because Vernon and some of the other veteran actors were doing hour-long TV dramas. All three of them thought Ned was going to cancel the movie right then. But instead he said, 'You know what, go make your fucking movie! Go ahead.'" When they got outside his office, Sean looked at John and said, 'We won.'"

Landis had long been a fan of Verna Bloom after seeing her in such films as *Medium Cool* and *The Hired Hand*. She often played a tough broad, not unlike the hot, tough, boozing Marion Wormer, who, as much as the Deltas, was Dean Wormer's biggest problem.

The only other fairly well-known actor to be hired was Cesare Danova, who with his thick Italian accent, had been type-cast in a lot of Mafia roles. I had wondered why the writers had decided the mayor of the town of Faber had to have an Italian accent, but I never objected or got a straight answer.

Now Chinich really had to get to work. Next we needed the Omegas and the Deltas who would party with Belushi. Chinich worked in both New York and LA interviewing and reading thousands of applicants. He remembers when he first saw Stephen Furst. Stephen did a monologue that brought tears to his eyes. "He was really good. I knew he would be Flounder right away."

Stephen was a graduate of Virginia Commonwealth

University. Afterward, he remembers, "I had to decide whether I wanted to go to New York or LA to be a starving actor. I decided the weather was better out in LA so I drove there. I had just gotten married and our honeymoon was in a U-Haul truck. Believe it or not, I know it's parodied in a lot of movies but I actually had a Gremlin X and we towed my Gremlin X behind a U-Haul truck cross-country from Virginia to LA, and that was our honeymoon. I got a job delivering pizzas while I tried to figure out how to get into the movies."

He had a problem. He didn't have an agent and he wasn't a member of the Screen Actor's Guild. So he went to the Guild and became friends with one of the people who worked there. She suggested he try to get a new agent, since he had had no luck with the established agents. "How do I know who the new ones are?" he asked. She handed him a list. "Here are ten brand-new agents. They just signed up with the Guild, so they should be anxious to get new clients."

Stephen tried to contact the agents, but only two of them would take his call. He explains what happened next. "One of the two was a woman who looked exactly like Tina Turner and her agency was called the Glam More Agency. I went into her office and she said, 'Can you take your watch and ring off and put them in the middle of my desk?' I was thinking, this is strange, but I really, really wanted an agent, so I took my watch and ring off and put them in the middle of her desk. She put her hands out and started moving them around my stuff. 'Okay,' she said. 'You can put your ring and watch back on. I got signals that we can make money together.' And I said, 'Well, thank you very much, I appreciate it.' She said, 'You have to get some head shots and I have a photographer.' Like I didn't realize she was getting a kickback. So, I passed. I went to the second interview and it was a woman who was working above a flower shop and I signed with her and she arranged the audition for *Animal House*.

"I had six auditions for *Animal House* over a period of three months. I had a feeling they might have liked me but nothing happened. After every audition, I wouldn't hear anything for a while, maybe a week or two, until I would get a call and there would be somebody new in the room, either a Universal executive or [Matty], and then at the last audition, it was John Landis. After the read-through, I went to hand back my script to Chinich and he said, 'No. Keep it.' I asked if I had gotten the part but he couldn't tell me yet, that he didn't know. That was on a Friday. So, I worked at my pizza delivery job, as usual, and on Monday he called me and said that I had gotten the part. That was in September [1977] and I still had to wait a month before we started shooting, so I couldn't just take off. I continued to deliver pizza and told everyone I was starring in a movie for Universal but of course no one believed me.

"The next time I travelled was in a first-class seat on a plane to Eugene, Oregon."

Michael Chinich says that when they looked through the piles of photographs that had been submitted to them, before auditioning some of the younger Deltas and Omegas, they stopped when they came to a picture of Kevin Bacon. They agreed that this was the smarmiest looking kid they'd seen in any of the photos. He would be perfect for the role of Chip, the Omega pledge.

Kevin describes the newness and the excitement and the bewilderment of being nineteen and called in for your first film audition: "I'd just graduated high school in Philadelphia a couple of years before and I was working as a waiter at a restaurant and bar on the Upper West Side in New York. I was also going to the Circle in the Square acting school. One day, some people showed up at the school and told us they were looking for an actor for this *Lampoon* movie they were working on. They looked at us and for some reason they picked me out, said I looked right for the part. I had no idea what that meant but gave them my photo and made an appointment to see Michael Chinich. I didn't know what I was doing but I met him and read a couple of lines. In what seemed to be a few minutes, he said, 'Okay. Oh, if you get the part you'll have to cut your hair.' I said, 'Sure.' My hair was really long but hey, a haircut for a part in a movie.

"A couple of days later, I came back to my apartment and my roommate said, 'Some guy named Chinich from *Animal House* called. You got the part but it only pays scale.'

"I couldn't care less what it paid. I didn't even know what scale was. So, the next day I called Chinich and he said, 'We need you [on set] right away. You've got to leave tomorrow.'

'I said, 'But I've got a date.'

'He said, 'Tomorrow. You leave tomorrow.'

'And I said, 'But my laundry's out.'"

•   •   •

In the film, Bruce McGill, as D-Day, plays the don't-give-a-damn character, who became an icon for young people who yearned to be the dark silent hero on a motorcycle, who ignored rules imposed by the establishment, who could miraculously turn a sleek sedan into the ominous Deathmobile, and whose last known address was "unknown."

Shortly after the film came out, a syndicated cartoon was carried around the country that showed McGill in a vest, helmet, and so forth walking into a movie theater where *Animal House* was playing. Watching him are three obviously college-age students. One of them says to the other, "You know, we're just like him."

In the movie McGill was an island unto himself. He teamed up with the others, but always seemed to be on the outside, occasionally looking in. He was D-Day and no one else was like him.

He almost didn't get the job. McGill recalled, "I auditioned for John Landis. He had a list of all the actors they were considering for each part. D-Day was a hard part to reach for: I had to roar up on a motorcycle, hop off, and say a funny line. I did, and John wasn't impressed. He joked later that I gave the worst reading ever. He scratched me off the list. I didn't find out until much later how I got the part. When they started casting they found that they had crossed off all the actors who'd read for D-Day. Then John realized it was a hard part to read for. He said, 'Well, who's the best scratched-out actor?' He remembered me from some other things and I got the role."

•   •   •

Peter Riegert was a happy man at the time. He was living in Greenwich Village with Bette Midler, whom he had met only months before. He was making about $150 a week, but his rent was about $125 a month, so he was flush. And in his words, "I was in love and I was making a living. I was paying my bills. I thought that surely it would become more than this but it couldn't become better than this. Being in love and loving what you do, that's heaven."

In 1977 Peter was appearing in a play at the Cherry Lane Theater, written by a new playwright out of Chicago named David Mamet. It was called *Sexual Perversion in Chicago,* and he appeared in it for about eight months. (The play later became the movie *About Last Night,* with Demi Moore and Rob Lowe.) He was also part of an improv group called War Babies, so named, obviously, because almost all of the cast had been born right after World War II.

That same year he traveled to Los Angeles to meet up with Bette. War Babies was there as well, so he had work. The group had a big cast so he could take time off to do plays or films or television, and still come back and fit right in. One of the TV shows he did was *M*A*S*H.* Peter remembers he played a character named Igor but doesn't remember exactly what Igor did. But he liked working on the Fox lot and recalls that for about four days' work he was paid $250.

Just about that time, he was sent the *Animal House* script. "I remember literally falling out of bed when the horse gets killed. That's the one thing that truly convulsed me. I mean, I was laughing all the way through and I got it. I mean, I had been to college. I was an English major at the U of Buffalo and graduated in 1968. I wasn't in a fraternity but always felt that I could find the value in things that other people couldn't and I knew that was how I was going to make my call. I would either find something that other people turned down or get lucky and it'd be between me and someone else. So my memory is I auditioned first with Tim Matheson and we improvised around the dildo scene, coming up with names for the dildo.

"I gave Landis a copy of a short film I did in New York, the only film I had of myself, called *A Director Talks about His Film*, which is about an Italian director talking in gibberish Italian, kind of like a Bertolucci character waxing philosophic about moviemaking. Totally nonsensical, but a lot of fun. I invited Michael Chinich to see War Babies. I wanted this fucking job, so I knew it was an important night with the group but it was only a so–so night. Chinich didn't hold that against me and Landis didn't think much of the film, but he didn't hold that against me either. I read with the two women that they were deciding on for Katy. I remember Karen Allen because it was very clear to me that she was the one. She emanated light. I mean, she was like a bulb that gave off this energy and she had that quality of not giving a shit, which Katy has to have. Anyway, lo and behold, I get the job. Why me? I always ask myself that whenever I get a job, but I had no clue, other than I had the requisite disregard for authority. It just was a great match, that part and me. You know, as a director now, I can tell you what I look for and it's not acting talent necessarily. It's who's right for the role."

Peter, being the dry, "anything goes" character, teamed

perfectly with Matheson, who played the charmer and the decision maker. That those two worked together so well was vital. It was as if they knew what the other was thinking. In the scene in which they discuss getting back at Wormer and Belushi goes off about the "Germans' bombing Pearl Harbor," Peter and Tim look at each other and we know: It's retribution time.

When Karen Allen was eighteen, she went to the Fashion Institute of Technology. She was interested in clothing design as a career, but after a couple of years, like most college students, she went down a different road. She decided to take some time off and worked at the Washington Theater Laboratories in Washington, D.C. In 1976 she went to New York to study at the Lee Strasberg Institute.

One day as she was leaving Strasberg, she saw a three-by-five card posted on the bulletin board that read "Feature film casting! College-aged actors and actresses needed! Bring picture and résumé."

She wrote down the information in her notebook, got the headshot and résumé made, went to the audition, and took a number. A few days later they called her back.

Karen recalls, "I got there and one of the casting people rushed up to me and said, 'I know you don't have an agent and you're not in the union but you're coming in to meet John Landis because you're the one I want for the role.' I did meet John, and then they wanted me to go to Los Angeles because no one had ever heard of me and the people at Universal were, I guess, dubious. I went to LA, auditioned, and then I had to get on the plane not knowing if I got the part. Michael Chinich called and all he said was, 'I'm going to give you the names of four agents.' I called and left messages for all four of them and I heard from no one. Chinich kept calling me, 'Do you have an agent? You gotta get an agent! We want to negotiate your contract.' I was stunned. I had actually gotten a job. Finally, Joan Hyler called me. She was at ICM and she had just become an agent. I went to her office the next day. We hit it off and she became my agent."

Karen echoed Peter Riegert's feeling of confidence: "I knew I was right for the role, I totally related to it. Like so many in the film, we were perfect matches. I felt I matched the role and also felt I had matched up well on screen with Peter. You know Katy, she's really trying to pull Boone out of that madhouse. When we meet them—I think it's one of the first moments on film—she's flipping him the bird and she leaves the house. It's just one of those great relationships because there's something kind of sweet in the way they're not getting along because they obviously adore each other but he wants to hang with his buddies."

A stable of actors was coming together. But we were nowhere near done.

11

FINDING MORE ANIMALS

As Michael Chinich recalls, "John Landis and I argued continually about casting the role of Pinto. I had seen Tom Hulce on Broadway in *Equus* and I thought he was incredible. Landis didn't think he was good-looking enough but I insisted that the kid was a great young actor and would be perfect as the innocent bewildered Pinto, who at first had no idea what he was getting into and little by little started to *like* what he got into.

"We kept interviewing other actors, never finding anyone we liked, and I kept coming back to Hulce. Finally, I convinced Landis to come and see him in the play. When we walked out, he turned to me and said, 'You were right. He's perfect for Pinto.'

"It was truly amazing," Chinich says, "how we seemed to get all the right people for the right roles. We saw so many actors: endless Pintos and Flounders, even Omegas. For the Omegas, we just kept looking for nasty and smarmy—we wanted wiseasses! The actors we got weren't really nasty or smarmy or wiseasses but they could play it."

Tim Matheson was a well-known child actor, probably best known for the TV series *The Virginian*. As a young adult, he played the villain in Clint Eastwood's *Magnum Force*, the first sequel to *Dirty Harry*.

As Otter he was one of the actors everybody felt strongly about right from the beginning of auditions. Otter was handsome, funny, and smart as hell. That was Matheson. His ready wit showed particularly well when he read with Riegert and Mary Louise Weller, who would play Mandy Pepperidge. If there's such a thing as a role of a lifetime, it was Matheson's turn as Otter. He had never before, and never since, fit a role so perfectly.

Mark Metcalf, who played Niedermeyer, is probably one of the most easygoing guys you'll ever meet, but he was deadly mean on screen. He originally came to the casting sessions to audition for the role of Otter. Metcalf read so well, there was a good deal of talk about him, and when it was finally decided that Matheson seemed to be perfect for Otter, Metcalf could play Niedermeyer, who like Dean Wormer was a true villain. We had to see if he could get that nasty. The Niedermeyer character epitomized to the writers, to all of us, the Nixon flunky who would do anything, literally anything, for his boss and his cause.

Before auditioning for the movie, Metcalf had acted in only one other film, *Julia*. In it, he had a good one-on-one scene with Jane Fonda. Then, ten days before the movie opened, he got a call from an executive at Fox who told him they had to lose twenty minutes, and his big scene ended up on the cutting room floor. He tried to reassure Metcalf by telling him they also had to trim scenes of a young new actress who was on everyone's radar screen, Meryl Streep. (Metcalf's name is still in the credits of the film.)

When he auditioned, he really wanted the role of Otter, the guy who got all the girls. "I thought that would be a cool part to play," he recalled. "But John Landis took one look at me and said, 'Do you know how to ride?' And I said, 'Yeah, of course I know how to ride. I was practically born on a horse. My mom and dad lived in Montana and when my mother was pregnant, her water broke while they were out riding one day and she just slid off the horse and gave birth to me right there in the grass, right next to the horse.'

"John just stared at me and said, 'Yeah, right.' So I told him five more lies about how I knew how to ride a horse and he nodded at each one and said, 'Yeah, right,' and finally said, 'All right, get out of here.'

"A couple of days later he called me and said, 'Okay, listen, I want you to do this Niedermeyer part but you're gonna have to audition for the guys in suits.'"

"It was so much fun," he said, "because I read with Chinich and hit him with my script a bunch of times.

"I got a call the next day and they said, 'Okay, they liked it, they want you.' 'Okay,' I said, 'now can you get me some money so I can learn how to ride a horse?'"

The character of Niedermeyer is one that moviegoers remember to this day.

Another character that remains with us is Babs, as

played by Martha Smith. Martha was, she recalls, "struggling like most young actresses. I had this funny agent—I don't know if he's with us anymore—he was an older guy and I think his wife was one of the original Ziegfeld girls. When I did leave him for APA, I called to tell him I was leaving. He said loudly, "Marsha! You can't leave us! We got you that Animal Farm movie." I think that was a good indication it was time for me to move on.

"When I first read the script I wanted to audition for the role that Mary Louise Weller ended up getting, Mandy. I was, however, a little apprehensive. She plays a pretty long nude scene in the picture, the one with Belushi on the ladder peering at her while she undresses. But it didn't matter, it was decided that I would do Babs, the comedy role, and certainly it helped launch my career, as I did a lot of comedy after that. And Babs is a more memorable character because she is funny and silly, and truly an Omega, whereas the Mandy character was more normal, and did have a feeling for Otter and eventually for Bluto as well."

At every high school or college, there's always one girl who seems so damned gorgeous and unobtainable that you figure she'll never be interested in you. In *Animal House*, Mandy Pepperidge, as played by Mary Louise Weller, was just that girl. And, as was probably true of all of those unobtainable girls, Mandy was obtainable, at least to some incredibly lucky guy. She was the perfect coed, beautiful, smart, and cool.

Jamie Widdoes as Hoover, the Delta president, was on target. He had graduated from NYU's Tisch School of Arts in 1976, only a year before he auditioned for the movie. While waiting to hear if he'd gotten the *Animal House* role, he appeared in several New York stage plays, including *Wonderful Town*. I remember watching him in an audition: He acted with cautious self-control. He seemed to know what he was doing but maybe wasn't completely sure. He was simply Hoover, all arms and legs, all of them moving wildly. He would complain, then stop, and think, "Well, maybe we could do that." The character was smart but because of all the parties and goings-on with the Deltas, he failed at his schoolwork, although he probably got the highest marks in the fraternity. He was in charge, but in name only. Otter was probably the true leader and Bluto led them into madness. Hoover was the hapless ringmaster who valiantly tried, but failed, to keep the animals under control.

James Daughton's portrayal of Omega president Greg Marmalard was utterly on target. At his audition, his reading of the role was so good, I remember turning to Ivan and saying, "Didn't you just hate this guy when you were in school?" And you did, and of course, that was the idea.

Belushi's wife, Judy, makes two uncredited appearances in the film, one when she dances with John to "Shout!" at the toga party and the other when she sits on the staircase as Bluto smashes Stephen Bishop's guitar.

Bishop was another who came to the movie as an "FOL," or Friend of Landis. He would eventually write the theme song for the movie. The song that Bishop sings as Bluto walks down the stairs, "I Gave My Love a Cherry," is more than 600 years old. We picked it because we had no money left to pay additional music royalties, and being that old, the song is in the public domain. It also was the perfect song to elicit Bluto's reaction, the smashing of the guitar that was a complete surprise to Bishop, who admitted later that it freaked him out.

The most memorable entrance I've heard about in Hollywood was that made by Danny DeVito, then relatively unknown, when he came in to read for the role of Louis in the television show *Taxi*. The character was a mean little guy who sat behind a cage all day long and barked out orders and insults to his underlings. DeVito entered the room and considered the line-up of producers and directors sitting there, including the legendary writer and director James L. Brooks. He stared for a long beat and then raised the script high above his head in anger and slammed it to the ground. "Who wrote this shit?" Everyone in the room broke out in laughter. He got the role.

The actor DeWayne Jessie, who had the role of musician Otis Day, had an equally engaging entrance at his audition. He wanted to make sure we knew he could sing, so he entered the office singing. In most auditions, as was the case in nearly all of the *Animal House* auditions, actors sit quietly, chat with each other, or read script pages that have been given to them while waiting to read. But DeWayne was sure to make an entrance.

Before *Animal House*, DeWayne had appeared in *Car Wash* and *The Bingo Long Traveling All-Stars & Motor Kings*. The band that accompanied him, The Knights, was actually a touring group called Chris Holmes and the Commandos, who were brought to the film by Robert Cray, the great jazz musician who also played with them in the toga scene. We knew that DeWayne Jessie could act but he wanted to make sure we knew he could sing.

And so, with these important pieces of the puzzle in place, we were very nearly ready to make a movie. Now all we needed was a place to shoot.

12

GETTING THERE

So now we had a director, the cast, and a crew. As the film's coproducer, I'd be travelling between the *Lampoon* offices in New York, the film's location, and meetings at the studio. Ivan would be on the set throughout the shoot and would also double as second unit director, which would be a step up for him toward his enormously successful career as a director. (His comedies would be outdone in box office success possibly only by those of another *National Lampoon* alum, John Hughes.)

Our next job: location. We knew that we wanted to shoot on the grounds of a real university, getting not only college buildings and classrooms as exteriors but also the students as our extras. Universal's location people started contacting various schools across the country and in most cases they were immediately turned down. The University of Missouri thought about it for a while, then asked to read the script, and like actor Jack Webb and many of the directors we approached, they passed.

Finally, William Beaty Boyd, the president at the University of Oregon in Eugene started thinking about it seriously. Some years earlier, while a senior administrator at a California university, he had passed on a picture, and had regretted it. The film was *The Graduate*, so he wanted to think this one over carefully. Ultimately, he agreed, but only with the stipulation that the University of Oregon would never be mentioned in the film. As a matter of fact, in one scene the state flag is seen and it's not that of the state of Oregon, but of New Mexico, which the designer thought had a better look. We were given thirty days on campus to shoot, which meant we would have to schedule a six-day week.

With a location settled, equipment, designers, carpenters, and painters all moved into Eugene, Oregon's second-largest city, sitting in the western part of the state. A large chunk of the more than 100,000 people who live there are students or faculty of the University of Oregon. The nearby town of Cottage Grove agreed to serve as the location for the parade at the end of the film, although part of that scene was eventually finished on the Universal lot in Burbank.

Ivan remembers the young Landis: "He was very professional and I thought he had a real comedic sensibility. It was somewhat different from the actual screenplay in that he came from a broader place. The humor in the script was sort of really college based. Landis never got out of high school and there was a kind of disconnect in terms of the writers' edgy humor. I mean, the one thing about *Animal House* was that it really changed the comedic language. Before *Animal House* they were all watching Bob Hope and Phyllis Diller and Dean

Belushi and Landis in a rare quiet moment for both of them.

Tim Matheson (Otter) as he delivers his defense of Delta excesses.

Peter Riegert and Karen Allen: The Boone / Katy romance that reminded everyone that college, like "knowledge," is good.

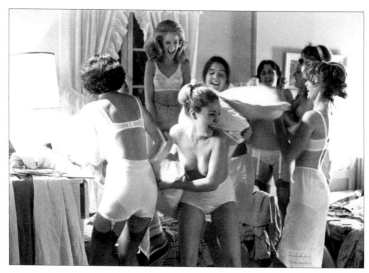

Pillow fight!

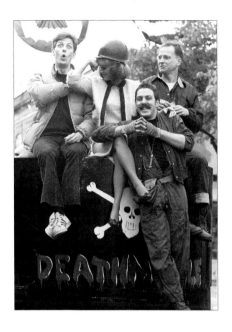

On the Deathmobile at the parade (from left to right) Chris Miller, Mary Louise Weller, Bruce McGill, and Doug Kenney. Mary Louise played the beautiful Mandy Pepperidge. Screenwriter Miller also played the Delta, Hardbar.

Doug Kenney, Matty Simmons, Ivan Reitman, and Chris Miller on the last day of the shoot.

Left to right: Bruce McGill (D Day), Tim Matheson (Otter), Karen Allen (Katy), James Widdoes (Hoover), and Stephen Furst (Flounder), "speaking" Delta House sign language.

Sarah Holcomb (Clorette) and Tom Hulce (Pinto): the only virgins in the movie.

Omegas clowning offscreen: Kevin Bacon (Chip), Mark Metcalf (Niedermeyer), and James Daughton (Marmalard).

Stephen Furst (Flounder) on the receiving end as Landis bombards him with groceries.

The Deltas, all drunk, being told they're getting kicked out of school. What follows is Flounder throwing up "on" Dean Wormer.

Professor Jennings (Donald Sutherland) explains why "evil" is good.

Director John Landis checks to make sure that Kevin Bacon will be "in the ground" during the parade chaos.

Verna Bloom and John Vernon (Vernon and Marion Wormer) spending a quiet night at home.

Offscreen party time at Delta House. McGill, Belushi, Furst, and Matheson. The good times didn't stop when the camera did.

John Belushi: *This* is a Greek god?

Martin and Jerry Lewis. It was the fifties generation turning its creative approach over to the baby boomers, with maybe the exception of *M*A*S*H,* which was kind of in between *Animal House* and the earlier comedies.

"There really had been no film that had the language of *Animal House* and even though it was set in 1962, it was made in the seventies and was much more reflective of that kind of attitude and language and behavior. It was the language of the college students of the day and most important, of the *National Lampoon.* The *Lampoon* was the first publication to capture this voice, and that was what was great about it. Landis's job was to turn this into a studio picture and he was up to it. He was brought up on the Three Stooges, Abbott and Costello, and comedies which were really from a generation earlier, but he was smart enough to know a good thing and a good script when he saw it. His comedic instinct happily mixed well with what the writers had given him. He made it somewhat broader than what had been written, and that captured the audience, along with the cleverness, the attitudes, and the philosophies of the script. He had us, he had writers on the set, and he had actors who had good ideas, and as we approached production he did a last polish to accommodate the realities of shooting and to incorporate some of his new ideas and those from the cast."

Ivan and Landis, like many of the key crew members, had arrived in Eugene early. But about two weeks before production began, his wife, Genevieve, gave birth to their first child in Toronto and he left to be with them. The child was Jason Reitman, now one of the most highly regarded directors in Hollywood. When Ivan returned, he returned with his wife and the baby.

In his further reflections on the film, Ivan has said that Landis's directorial technique was very fraternal. He almost ran the cast like it was a fraternity and he was the fraternity leader. And the fact that many in the cast, including the extras and others involved in the production, had been frat members, including the Delta and Omega fraternities, lent an authenticity to the production. Shooting on an active college campus in the fall, on fraternity row, gave it a sense of reality too.

In the days before shooting, the actors started to arrive. Peter Riegert remembers his adventures on the way to Eugene. "We were all supposed to meet at Universal at seven in the morning," he recalled, "so Bette drove me to Universal but somehow we couldn't find where we were supposed to meet. We didn't have cell phones back then but I knew we were leaving from LAX, so Bette took me there. This now was almost a little less than a week before we started shooting and I got lost before I got found and I was like, 'Holy shit! How could I?' Because I was really excited. This was going to be a big deal. I sat beside Stephen Furst on the flight and I remember he'd never flown before. He thought the tray that folds down was where the movie on the flight was going to be played. He was so young and so naïve. And then we arrived in Eugene and went out to the Roadway Inn and spent a week basically getting into trouble and getting haircuts."

Stephen Furst remembers the trip to Eugene as well. "I

was in the airport in LA and I saw this blue Jaguar pull up and Peter Riegert came out and the person he hugged was this bright orange–haired girl and she looked so familiar. And then on the plane with Riegert I said, 'Peter, it's so funny. I saw you pull up at the curbside at the airport and when you got out of the car I could have sworn that was Bette Midler, and when I saw it was you I realized it couldn't have been.' He laughed and told me it was Bette Midler and that she was his girlfriend. So from start to finish, I was Flounder, naïve, innocent, and bewildered."

He remembers when he first met Tom Hulce. Hulce was one of the more experienced actors in the film. He had done movies before and starred in *Equus*, which Stephen had seen on Broadway while he was a college student. During the casting process, Michael Chinich had called Stephen and asked him if he knew an actor named Thomas Hulce, and Stephen excitedly asked, "The guy from *Equus*?" Chinich told him that we were thinking of pairing Hulce with Stephen so we'd have Flounder and Pinto, the two college freshman. "I told Chinich that Hulce was terrific," Stephen says, "and then I got really nervous because I was going to act with a guy I'd just been admiring nine months before on Broadway."

All the actors who played Deltas remember what first bonded them while in Eugene—a big fight at the jock fraternity. The cast had wandered into a campus party at this particular frat house. They had yet to start rehearsals but had had dinner together, during which they sparred in typical actor style—how each one was going to outdo the other and come out the star of the film. But that had been done, like an athlete going into a football game, as a means to get adrenaline going. The performance was the thing.

After dinner, Tim Matheson, Karen Allen, Bruce McGill, Jamie Widdoes, and Peter Riegert went, uninvited, to a U of O frat party. Suffice it to say, the fraternity members didn't like them. They felt that they were intruders and they particularly didn't like the way the college girls were taken with Matheson and the other guys. They started threatening them, words were exchanged, and a group of very large jocks started pushing and then hitting them. At one point Matheson was on the ground with a crowd of frat boys towering over him, kicking and punching. Widdoes, in true Hoover style, tried to reason with them, but one of the men threw a punch and knocked out a tooth.

Karen started screaming when she saw both Tim and McGill on the ground being pummeled. Peter grabbed her and tried to get her out through the front door but she tore away from him and ran back to the fight and started screaming at them. Somehow, they all escaped.

Now, battered and bruised, they were back at the Roadway Inn. As they sat there nursing their wounds, Cliff Coleman, the first assistant director, opened the door and stuck his head in. "I told you when you first got here," he said, "you guys gotta stay out of trouble. You think you're hot shit but you're just a bunch of Hollywood pussies and you'd better behave yourself, 'cause this is not your town."

After that, he took them to the hospital to be patched up. Riegert had bleeding in his ear, McGill had a mouse under his eye, and Widdoes's tooth turned out to be only chipped and was repaired. They sat in Tim's room until something like 2 A.M. that Sunday morning, when Cliff Coleman again entered the room. Cliff is about six foot four and he was backlit so that he looked like a figure out of a Clint Eastwood movie, and he just stood there, looked at the group, and shook his head. "I told ya," he said, "you're just a bunch of Hollywood pussies."

Happily, the next day was a Sunday and they had the day off to sit around laughing about what had happened. They started to realize that they were now, in a way, their own fraternity. The jock fight had brought them together. Later in the day, Belushi arrived from New York, where he had been doing *Saturday Night Live,* and they told him about the fight. He wanted to go back to the frat house and kept saying, "We gotta go back, we gotta get those guys!"

"I mean," Riegert says, "it was like the script. But we said, 'Are you out of your fucking mind? We're outnumbered and they're bigger than we are. This is the biggest jock fraternity.'" Belushi thought that over, 'Well,' he said, 'we'll get the Teamsters and we'll go back and beat the shit out of them.' And Belushi kept trying to organize us, trying to convince us we had to go back to protect whatever dignity we had left but none of us were ready for that and we ended it merely by saying, 'You're crazy.'"

Karen Allen laughed while recalling the fight. "I screamed so much at the guys who were kicking Bruce and Tim that I literally had no voice for the next couple of days. Fortunately, I didn't have to shoot right away but I was screaming the whole time this was going on, trying to get them to stop."

So now the bonding was starting to take place once again. Riegert had met Belushi during *Lemmings* but hadn't met Hulce yet. McGill had done a film in New York and he'd met Peter there because they were both mutual friends of the actor John Heard.

Good-naturedly, they sniped at each other. Peter described it as the gunfight at the O.K. corral. "And the great thing about good actors is they don't defer. A good actor takes the part. It's one thing to be given a part, but unless you take hold of that part, you can't do anything with it."

So everybody at the table was pretty much saying "You're not gonna get by me." Which was how they'd been feeling since they first got there. Now, however, they were starting to become close teammates—so important because acting, particularly in an ensemble movie, is collaborative, not competitive. Something else happened the following Monday that brought the Deltas even closer together.

They all had to get haircuts. John Landis had flown a hairdresser up from LA and the first person to get his hair cut was Jamie Widdoes. The rest of the Deltas were in an outside room with Landis when the woman hairdresser came back with Jamie in tow. Landis took a look at the haircut and said, "Thanks a lot. Gee, I'm not really sure about this." She didn't seem to be sure about it herself. "Well," she answered, "I just got here and I'm a little tired, maybe I can touch something up a little later." Landis stood up and put a hand on her shoulder. "You're tired," he said with feeling. "Why don't you go back to your room and relax and take it easy." When she left, John called in an assistant and said, "Fire her. We've gotta get someone who can cut hair from 1962." They found an Italian barber in Eugene who knew how to do "Detroit," who knew how to do sides. "Well," according to Riegert, "we all looked at Jamie's haircut and feared for the worst. So we got drunk and went to this barber shop and sat around for a couple of hours as this new barber gave us these severe haircuts."

Hairdressing for the actresses in the movie was even more challenging. Martha Smith, whose 1962-style coiffeur took hours to style, still feels that hair stylist Marilyn Phillips should have gotten an Academy Award for her work on those period re-creations.

The actors cast as Omegas never knew what hit them. The Deltas had arrived in Eugene a week before the Omegas. Mark Metcalf [Niedermeyer] was the first Omega to arrive at the business office across from the hotel. When he got there they told him that Landis wanted to see him at the dining room at the Roadway Inn. Eagerly, Mark sprinted across the street and walked into the motel and the dining room. As he did, he saw Landis sitting in a corner surrounded by the actors who would be playing Deltas. As he neared the table, Landis jumped up, pointed to him, and yelled, "It's Niedermeyer! Get him!" With that said, the Deltas at the table started throwing food at Niedermeyer. It was the food fight before the food fight scene.

What Landis was doing, and what he accomplished during the actual shoot, was to make sure the actors who were to play Deltas genuinely did not like the Omegas.

Kevin Bacon would play Chip, the Omega freshman pledge. He had been told by Chinich on short notice that he had to rush to Eugene, and he rushed. He left the next day after getting the call and, right off the bat, he was in heaven. He flew first-class for the first time in his life. (He didn't even know that you got free drinks.) He was then picked up at the airport and rushed to the set to meet Landis. The first thing Landis said to him was "You need a haircut." So they took him to the Italian barber who cut off nearly all of Kevin's hair.

After the haircut he went back to the set and sat around for a week—this after being told he had to be there immediately. He remembers calling his roommate and telling him to pick up his laundry and to call the girl he had the date with to tell her he couldn't make it.

I had stressed from the outset that there had to be a clear distinction between the good guys and the bad guys. John Vernon certainly epitomized the bad guy, but the character Niedermeyer took it even farther. He was a truly bad cat.

"Well, John set it up real nicely," Metcalf recalls, "having the Deltas arrive in Eugene earlier than the Omegas, and of course, I was the first who learned we were in for a month of war. John drew the line between the Deltas and the Omegas and had us at each other's throats all the time, but we were actors and we knew it was a good idea. I moved my hotel room to one over McGill's so I wouldn't be able to get any sleep, because they were all partying there, almost every night. I'd sit there spit-polishing my boots and studying my lines and cursing and getting madder and madder and madder—doing it all in the Method actor style. I knew I couldn't go down to the party because I didn't want to be around those guys. I had to hate them. I had to have my edge. It wasn't easy for me at all when I realized that basically I was an Omega and most of the other people were Deltas or were rooting for them. It was a good idea and by the time we showed up, everybody was kind of disdainful of us, so we hung out together and our hate for them festered even further, as John expected."

Martha Smith says, "It was more or less like the opening scene, with Stephen sniffing his armpits—you know, is there something wrong with me? But the idea was right on. The animosity we felt for each other during the shoot clearly showed on the screen. My character was totally down on the Deltas and the feeling was mutual."

We had our director, cast, and crew. We had the two warring armies ready to do battle and the place to film that war. It seemed it had taken forever to get the movie green-lighted—and then just the briefest blink of time to get it shot.

13

SHOOTING THE ANIMALS

And then, the shoot. Everybody has memories from those thirty-two days and these include recollections of the precision with which we went from start to finish. Reitman says that it went without a hitch, mostly because everyone was so well prepared and anxious to do things right. Everything was shot on time and, as the picture moved along, everybody, cast and crew, even day players, seemed to get into it. It became a cause. They were going to make this damn little movie and make it perfect and everybody felt that way. Usually on a movie set the key players are excited while day players and extras and many members of the crew are just there to make a buck. It didn't feel this way on *Animal House*. It seemed like everybody knew they were doing something that they would all remember, something that would be important and sustaining.

There was no studio interference, except for the equipment. The studio charged the picture for using their equipment and we had a big fight because we didn't want their cameras.

So we got Panavision cameras, but the head of the sound department wanted us to use his stuff. John Landis got sound man Bill Kaplan into the union so he could do the movie and he wanted to bring his own equipment, which was state-of-the-art stuff, but the studio absolutely refused.

"You must," the studio insisted, "use our equipment." And their equipment was old and beat-up, having been used again and again. The studio charges every movie for the use of their equipment so it's in their interest not to allow anyone else's. According to Landis, "The way Sid Sheinberg set up the studio was that every department was in competition and had to make their nut, so the movie was like everyone's thing to rape." John Lloyd, a great art director, who had an opening between major films and had read our script, had agreed to do the movie. He was not only much-honored in his field but he knew everything about dealing with the studio and helped us to avoid using equipment and materials that were below par.

Kaplan was upset with the radio microphones. He swore we were picking up police calls. So he announced that he would use his own equipment "for free." Because of that equipment, there are hardly any ADR [automatic dialogue replacement] postproduction recordings on the movie. Usually on a movie many of the spoken lines are redone in postproduction but not so for us.

One night, Landis was asleep and was woken by a phone call. "This guy from Universal. I didn't know who he was," Landis recalled. "Is this John Landis?" a voice asked.

When Landis told him it was, the voice said, "Listen, this

is Dick Stump, the head of the sound department at Universal, we watched the dailies from your show and there's a shot where the dean walks into the frat house and you can hear everything he says."

Bewildered, Landis asked, "Yeah? What's the problem?"

"The production sound is very good," he was told. "You must not be using our stuff." So Landis told him that they were using Bill Kaplan for sound and he was giving us his equipment at no charge and it was great. "Young man!" came the rejoinder, "I want you to use our equipment." Landis thought for a moment, then said, "You know what, FUCK YOU!" The next day Marshall Green, the head of practical production at Universal, called Landis and said, "John, you can't yell at department heads like that." Landis told him what had happened and Green just laughed.

Another example of the studio's demands for economy and the low status this film held was that the director never saw dailies. In those days, you printed each day's shoot and it was very expensive, so Universal printed only one set and they sent it to LA to show the executives. Landis recalls that film editor George Folsey was driving him crazy. "Every day I'd say, George, how's it look?" And George would reply with one-word answers.

Sean Daniel remembers those dailies. "After we began filming, it was just me and the postproduction guy watching the dailies in an empty screening room, when all of a sudden the word began to get out that something very funny was happening up in Eugene, Oregon. And Landis, as a prank, because he knew it would make everybody back in the studio lean on me, would pop up in front of the clapboard and say, 'Hi, Sean!' just as they were about to mark it.

"As the word began to spread around the production office that these dailies were funny, the screening room became more and more crowded. Everyday at two o'clock, the room would fill up and people started to laugh their asses off at what they were seeing."

A few days after they checked in to the Roadway Inn, Bruce McGill stood in the lobby studying a small piano that sat in the corner of the room. Hours later, after midnight, he and a couple of other Deltas went down to the lobby and very quietly wheeled the piano to the staircase and the four of them carried it up to Bruce's room.

The room became party central. It was *Animal House* during the day and a real-life animal house party room at night. What went on there included anything and everything. A lot of booze, a lot of pot, a lot of singing, a lot of sex. There was an occasional run-through of lines, but it was mostly partying. The Deltas had united and this was their bonding room. Mostly it was the regular crowd, the Deltas, with a lot of college girls. There were romances: It's said that Tom Hulce and Sarah Holcomb, who played the mayor's daughter, saw a lot of each other those nights. It's also said that the noise could be heard as far away as nearby motels, where Reitman and his wife and baby stayed.

But nobody complained. The townspeople of Eugene had taken this movie into their hearts. They seemed to feel, just as those who were more deeply involved with the production, that this was their movie and it was going to be great and they were going to do anything they could to make it great. If the actors wanted to go nuts at night, that would be fine. They never killed a horse or destroyed a parade.

There were a lot of pranks, though. One night, one of the University of Oregon professors dropped by for a drink, took off his shoes, and relaxed. At one point he got up to go to the bathroom and when he got back his shoes had been nailed to the floor.

Coed panties were collected and nailed to the walls as ornaments. Jamie Widdoes would often be seen doing his juggling act, Matheson would be on the prowl, McGill would be hammering away on the piano. The married people, like Chinich, Reitman, Belushi, and Furst showed up once in a while to have a drink.

The nights in Bruce's room took everybody's mind off the movie and made filming even better, because they showed up the next day not only ready but relaxed, actually a little tired. But psychologically, Bruce's room was as great for bonding as the fight at the frat house and the awful haircuts.

Reitman and his wife and baby went to John and Judy Belushi's that Thanksgiving. He still remembers that it was one of the best Thanksgivings he's ever spent. John, who was totally clean throughout the shoot, sober and ready to work at all times, was the perfect host, as was Judy. He was joined by the "Deltas" as well as Landis and other actors and crewmembers. "It was like family," Reitman says.

Few scenes were ad-libbed but when they were they were gems. The scene in the supermarket where Otter is throwing food to Flounder is a wonderful example of Landis's wacky sense of humor. Stephen remembers, "There was a piece of business in the script that says that Otter throws a bottle of Mazola corn oil at me and I catch it, but Landis just started throwing cans and packages at me, all the while screaming, 'Catch 'em, catch 'em, catch 'em!!' And I miraculously caught them. I don't know how I did it and I probably could never do it again. We only did one take on that so it was great."

Martha Smith remembers the only ad-lib she did in the film. It's in the cafeteria just before the food fight. She looks at the disheveled Bluto and declares in disgust, "That boy is a P-I-G, pig!"

In the Delta initiation scene, Flounder's face, as that of a perspective member, is projected onto a screen. The Deltas gathered in the room start throwing beer cans at the image. Hoover tries to explain that Flounder was a legacy student, but that doesn't seem to matter until Stork, the dork played by Doug Kenney, gives the ultimate reason for accepting him: "We need the dues!"

Perhaps one of Karen Allen's most memorable moments in the film is her "butt scene" with Donald Sutherland. "This was toward the end of the shoot," she said. "I had no idea that I'd be standing on the set completely naked. I'd never done anything like that before and I wasn't into doing it without any preparation at all. So Landis is trying to talk me into it and I'm digging in my heels and saying, 'No, it wasn't in the script,'" and Donald Sutherland is sort of leaning against the woodwork with a sly smile on his face and getting a huge kick out of this conversation. Finally, he comes over and says, 'Well,

John, if she's going to have to bare her buttocks, I should have to bare my buttocks too.' And Donald walks off the set and drops his trousers and comes back with a long sweater on and puts his hands down, grabs the bottom of the sweater to lengthen it, and covers the bare essentials. He walks through the scene like that and then turns and lifts up his arms as if he's looking above the refrigerator, looking for coffee or cereal. Everybody on the set cracked up, so I decided to go ahead and shoot it that way. I was completely taken with Donald's generosity, of his being willing to do this on my behalf to make me feel comfortable, so I just sort of relaxed and thought, okay, I'll do it. If he's gonna do it, I'll be happy to do it."

The cast was completely thrilled that Sutherland was doing the picture with them. The day that Donald appeared on the set to play Professor Jennings, they saw how he worked and how easy he made it seem. Sutherland's jaunty way of portraying the hip literature professor and his classroom explanation of what the poet Milton was trying to convey in his *Paradise Lost* was just simply superior acting. The admiration they had for him can be seen in the pot-smoking scene when Pinto is hanging on his every word.

Professor Jennings lights a joint and passes it around. "I won't go schizo, will I?" Pinto asks. Jennings smiles encouragingly and says, "There's a distinct possibility."

While stoned, Jennings would give his memorable, detailed explanation to Pinto about the relationship of the universe to an unseen speck on the tip of his finger. "Okay," Pinto says, "so that means our whole solar system could be like one tiny atom in the fingernail of some giant being. Which means, and this is the great part—that one tiny atom in my fingernail could be. . . ."

"A little tiny universe," agrees Jennings.

Hulce's reaction, as Pinto, to smoking pot for the first time, has always been, to me, one of the most brilliant moments of film comedy. His innocence just spilled over. The incredulity in Hulce's face was exceptional. He reacted with true wonderment, clearly identifying himself as an outstanding actor. And it was Sutherland's quiet, understated explanation that set up Hulce's reaction.

On the other hand, John Vernon's performance was so malevolent that he struck the "black hat" goal perfectly. The actors who played the three villains, Vernon, Metcalf, and Daughton, were easy and charming people on the set until they turned heinous in front of the camera. Like Sutherland and Verna Bloom, Vernon acted as a guide for the younger cast, advising them, answering questions, being steady not only for the actors but for the young director.

The last scene in the movie was the biggest and the hardest to produce: the parade scene. On the first day there were 4,000 extras crowding the streets of Cottage Grove. Landis had his schedule all set. He was going to shoot it in sequence. But the assistant director, Cliff Coleman, asked him, "What's the widest shot you have?"

John replied, "Well, it's when the riot breaks out and everyone is running in the streets screaming and the smoke is pouring out of the canisters and things are being broken and smashed and all hell breaks loose."

"Okay," Coleman said, "we gotta shoot that first."

When John asked why, Cliff explained, "We got four thousand people out there. If you want real chaos, you need all those people. We're only paying four hundred of them. The rest are there as sightseers and to be in a movie, but after lunch a bunch of them will leave, and tomorrow even fewer will come, and on the third day even fewer." John looked at him. Coleman had been an AD for years and knew how these things worked. They shot the mob scene on the first day. That afternoon, the crowd went from 4,000 to 3,000, the next day there were 2,000, and on the third day, after they'd shot all the mob scenes, there were 800 people there—even half of the people that were *being paid* didn't show up.

At Universal, George Folsey continued to edit the film as it came in each day. He recalls that he never had any doubt that the movie was going to be a hit. He read the script only a week before filming started. He had worked with Landis on *Kentucky Fried Movie* and felt that the script had a wonderful sense of camaraderie. "It was," he believed, "John's kind of movie. The Deltas were so strong and you really cared about them even though they were going to tear the school and the town apart. I just had a feeling it was going to be terrific. It wasn't an easy cut, you know, the movie was pretty long. The first cut was about three hours long. We took it down to about 165 minutes on the second cut, then we just kept whittling away at it and got it down to a couple of hours. I think finally the movie runs about 109 minutes."

On the last day of the thirty-two-day shoot, December 1, Peter Riegert and the other Deltas were filming their part of the parade scene in Cottage Grove. Bette Midler's birthday was that day, so he gathered everybody when they finished and they all sang happy birthday to her over the phone.

Karen Allen recalls her final day on the film. "I knew it was my last shot and I was overcome with emotion. Our budget was so tight that if it was your last day, you packed up all your stuff in the morning and brought it to the set and when you finished shooting they would whisk you away to the airport. There was no hanging around for a couple of days so that the studio would have to pay for room and food. They'd finished my shots in the parade scene and had another day or so for other shots. So I was there and I'd finished my last shot and Landis said, 'Okay, that's a wrap on Karen Allen.' I just burst into tears and Verna Bloom came up to me and threw her arms around me, laughing, and said, 'You'll remember the last day of your first movie for the rest of your life.' And I will."

Soon everyone and everything was wrapped. The fraternity house, once occupied by Phi Sigma Kappa and more recently abused as the set for our Delta House, was refurbished but remained unoccupied until it was torn down in 1986. Other sets on campus were removed and everything was again pristine. In nearby Cottage Grove workers were cleaning up the damage and garbage left after the parade scene. Eugene and Cottage Grove would soon be looking just like they did before we'd arrived.

When a movie shoot is over, everybody tells one another how much they loved working with them and they go on their way. Frequently there's a tear or two. But I've never since seen the sadness that I saw in those leaving the set of *Animal*

House. Perhaps it was because many of the actors and actresses were so new at filmmaking. To many, it was their first film-making experience and as it was for Karen Allen it was one they would live with for the rest of their lives. And indeed, unlike what happens on most shoots, even the Deltas and the Omegas—who became friends after the shoot ended—stayed in touch with one another. We've all attended numerous celebrations and awards and parties and many of us still meet up socially on a regular basis.

Landis doesn't agree with my belief that the bonding of the Deltas helped make the movie what it became. "The experience of making a movie," Landis has said, "doesn't have anything to do with how the movie turns out. I've worked on movies where everyone hated each other and the movie turned out great and I've worked on movies where everyone loved each other and the movie sucked." That may well be true, but there is no doubt in my mind (and certainly that mind is highly prejudiced) that this was a very special movie and the proof of what I say has been its longevity. People still talk about, dream about, and think about the work they did on *Animal House.*

To most of us, shooting the movie went like a blur. Belushi was coming and going. With the incredibly tight schedule we were on, everything had to be exact, and it was. For Landis, it was the movie of his life and he knew at every step what his very next step was going to be. The experience of veteran unit production manager Peter MacGregor Scott and first assistant director Cliff Coleman was exactly what Landis and the movie needed.

But it was the screenplay that was most responsible. It

was the tightest 110 pages of writing I had seen before or I have seen since, uncanny in the way the writers could foresee nearly every nuance and every twist and turn that would play out.

Now we had a film. It had to go through all the steps of post-production and then be sold to the public. They would decide if it all worked.

14

WHAT WE HAVE HERE IS A MOVIE

When shooting ended, Landis returned to Universal and started working with Folsey on the first cut. He was on deadline, as one always is during postproduction, so they worked well into the night. Finally, they had a rough cut and were ready to show it to the studio. Folsey describes it this way: "You know, the studio didn't quite know what to do with the movie. It had looked good in dailies but it was still, to most of them, a little movie. I guess they were happy that, for now, other people were dealing with it, and the execs rarely bothered to come over to the editing room to look at any cuts I'd been making while we were shooting, or after John had returned and was working on the rough cut. They pretty much left us alone until about a week before the preview in Denver. Ned Tanen called and wanted to see the rough cut.

"We had a mix by then, so the movie was pretty close to the final version. We all went into the screening room. There was Ned Tanen, John Landis, me, and Malcolm Campbell, my assistant. We were running the movie and we came to the scene where Otter is bringing roses over to the hotel where he thinks he's going to get laid. The door opens and the Omegas are in there and they whale the hell out of him. Ned watched this, then signals to an assistant to stop running the film. He turns to John and says, 'That's not funny!' John startles and pauses to think this over. Then he turns to me—and this was like John, who at that time was not sure how to handle someone like Tanen, and certainly neither was I. But John looked at me like, *What should I say?* So, I just shrugged and said, 'Well, it's not intended to be funny.' But, of course, it was very funny and was intended to bring the story along as well. So John turns back to Ned and says, 'Well, Ned, it's not intended to be funny.' Ned looks at him like he's lost his mind. 'Not intended to be funny?' he roars. 'We're making a comedy here and it's not intended to be funny?' Now, the movie resumed running and we all sat there in silence and watched it to the very end with nobody saying anything or even looking at each other. At the end of the screening Ned got up and turned to us. 'Nice job, boys,' he said. 'Hope it does well at the previews. See you in Denver.'"

So, on that inauspicious note, we all went to Denver. We flew up on the Universal corporate jet. There was Ivan, me, Tanen, Thom Mount, Sean Daniel, Landis, and Tanen's immediate boss, Sid Sheinberg.

The audience for the Denver screening had been, as most screenings are, selected to be the typical audience we hoped to market the movie to, so they were primarily young people.

What happened in Denver was the closest thing to the parade scene at the end of *Animal House* that I had ever seen. Never before or since had I seen a reaction to a film like I saw that evening. Audiences for years have been laughing and roaring and applauding when they watch *Animal House,* but not like in Denver.

At the end of the film, the audience literally stood on their seats and screamed. They threw popcorn in the air, they yelled in delight, they hugged each other. We were stunned, all of us. Even the veterans Sheinberg and Tanen looked at all of this with unbelieving eyes. The noise was tumultuous. Now people were running across aisles telling each other how much they loved the movie, how sensational it was, how much they had laughed. We sat there for nearly a half hour watching this. Then, as the audience filed out, we left by a side door and marched one by one to our waiting cars.

As we walked along, Tanen came up alongside me, put an arm around my shoulder, and asked, "What would you say if I asked you to take the black bar scene out? It's gonna get a lot of heat, you know."

I couldn't believe what I'd heard. I turned to him. "Are you crazy!?" I snapped. "Were you in that theater? Did you hear that audience? You'd be out of your fucking mind if you touch one moment in that movie. And let me tell you about the black bar scene. Blacks will love it. Nobody's going to complain about it except maybe one guy in the *Village Voice.*" (*The Village Voice* was, at that time, an extremely liberal weekly paper based in New York, and it criticized everything that came close to political incorrectness. I note here that when

Andrew Sarris reviewed it in the *Voice*, he didn't like the movie at all and took particular umbrage at the black bar scene. Of all the hundreds of reviews I've read, I saw no other negative reference to it.)

When I reacted the way I did, Tanen just smiled, shook his head, and said, "Okay," and we got into the car.

That was truly the night we won the war with Universal. From then on, they seemed to feel confident, almost certain, that we had done something extraordinary.

The next week we had another screening. This was a small test in Los Angeles at which a handpicked group of young people was shown the movie and then given cards to grade the film. The woman in charge of the testing went over the cards, then came over to the back of the room where I was sitting with Sean Daniel. "I've never seen anything like this," she said. "Ninety percent of these cards show excellent. We've never had a score as high as that before."

Sean looked at me and said, "We did it!"

The soundtrack for *Animal House* was a big departure from the soundtracks of earlier comedies. Landis came up with the idea of having a much more classical composer write a much more classical soundtrack. Instead of the usual bumps and jumps that accompany comedic moments in a movie and beg the audience to *laugh right now*, he wanted a composer who would almost make the movie seem like a drama. After much discussion with Reitman, who himself was a classical musician, Landis felt strongly that the movie should not be treated like a Laurel and Hardy film or *The Road to Morocco*. The soundtrack that was made was remarkably innovative.

Landis was friendly with Peter Bernstein, whose father, Elmer Bernstein, was one of the great film composers of the day. He'd won an Academy Award for *Thoroughly Modern Millie* but is perhaps remembered best for the score for *The Man with the Golden Arm,* one of the greatest film scores ever written. Through Peter, Landis got in touch with Elmer and asked him if he'd be interested. Bernstein's reaction was one of amazement. "Me?" he asked. "You want me to do a broad comedy?" Landis said we did. He sent Bernstein the script and a few days later Elmer agreed to do it. One should listen to the music in *Animal House* without watching the movie. It stands by itself as great entertainment. After *Animal House,* the Elmer Bernstein dramatic method of scoring a comedy took hold, and many comedies have since been scored that way.

The songs in the movie were mostly selected by Chris Miller with input from the studio and Reitman. Miller has always been an authority on sixties music and songs such as "Shout!," "Hey Paula," and "Wonderful World" had long since faded from popular culture but *Animal House* brought them back so resoundingly that they are still heard on television and radio and in crowded stadiums, where it's unusual to go to a football game and not hear "Shout!" played by one of the college bands.

Every University of Oregon game includes Steven Bishop's song "Animal House."

We bought the use of these songs for less than $100,000. Today each song on its own would cost more than that. *Animal House* and movies such as *American Graffiti* changed the price of song use in film both from publishers and performers and the costs are now ten to twenty times what they were in 1978.

The first trailer for the film was created while the movie was still in rough cut. It was a six-minute preview made for ShoWest, the annual convention of theater owners. Like the screening audiences in Denver and LA, the exhibitors were excited about the movie. That excitement, naturally, was not expressed in the same exuberant manner as the young crowd in Denver, but they liked it and they wanted it for their theaters.

An idea was developed for a trailer that would be attached to the start of one of Universal's movies and go into theatres all over the country. The trailer would open with me sitting at a desk. I would look up into the camera as a voice said, "Ladies and gentlemen, Matty Simmons, Chairman of the Board of the *National Lampoon*." I would then say, "It's with great pleasure that I announce that our first motion picture will be opening soon." As I finish my line, a huge klieg light drops from the ceiling, crashes into the desk in front of me, and destroys it, segueing into a collection of brief moments from the movie. John assured me that the fall of the klieg light would be calculated carefully and that I was in no danger of death or brain concussion. I agreed to do it.

Several days before it was to be filmed, I came down with a terrible cold. On the day of the filming, every aperture in my head was clogged. I was swallowing antihistamine pills by the hour. When I walked onto the sound stage at Universal, I was totally stoned. I barely heard Landis tell me not to be nervous, not to anticipate the klieg light, and above all, "Don't worry about a thing. We can do this in fifty takes if we have to."

After makeup, they led me to the desk and the camera rolled. Landis yelled, "Action!" and almost oblivious to what was going on around me, I recited my line. As I uttered the last word, the klieg light dropped and shattered the desk. I didn't move. I didn't blink. I was as calm as though nothing had happened. Landis was delighted. He ran up to me. "My God," he shouted. "That was great! You did it in one take. And I can't believe it but you didn't even blink when the goddamn light came down." I turned to him slowly and asked, "What'd you say?"

Around the same time, I was meeting with Charlie Powell and Buddy Young, going over advertising and marketing plans for the movie. I had worked closely with both of them when they were at Columbia Pictures promoting the film *The Man from the Diners Club*. We agreed that the illustrations that the studio had come up with didn't work and I recommended Rick Meyerowitz, a cartoonist who had become well-known particularly for his *Lampoon* cover painting of Mona Gorilla, to do the key art. Meyerowitz's illustration of the Deltas in front of their dilapidated frat house worked and is one of the most familiar pieces of art associated with a film.

At the *Lampoon*, we immediately started producing posters and T-shirts. The most successful one featured the key art on *National Lampoon Animal House* T-shirts with the quote on the back, "We can do anything we want. We're college students." The biggest-selling poster not only of the movie but in the country at that time had a picture of Bluto and the line "Blutarski for Senator." That poster sold tens of thousands.

Interestingly, the *Animal House* merchandise with the longest life was the navy sweatshirt that Belushi wore in the film. It simply reads COLLEGE. That sweatshirt is still sold on the *Lampoon* Web site as well as in stores all over the country. It remains one of the most popular sweatshirts ever produced.

The publicity and advertising campaigns were in place. It was time to let the critics and the public see this thing.

15

WHERE WERE YOU THAT NIGHT?

The world premiere was on July 24, 1978, two days before the film opened. Everybody wanted to be there and just about every celebrity in New York at the time was. We all arrived in Universal-supplied limousines. Stephen Furst reminisces: "I just remember how excited I was because we were a small movie and I don't think Universal or anybody knew that it was going to be the success that it was. For the premiere Universal had two actors assigned to one limousine. I had never ridden in a limousine before, unless somebody had died, and I was in the limo with Peter Riegert, and there was Bette Midler! Just nine months before, I had a poster of Bette Midler on my dorm room wall and there I was sharing a limousine with her and she was giving me instructions like, when you get out of the car, even though there'll be people asking for autographs, just keep walking, whatever you do, don't stop. I was polite and said okay, nobody's going to be asking me, nobody even knows who I am, and sure enough there were people asking for autographs.

"I had gone to a sneak preview in Westwood, in Los Angeles," Furst continues. "I was driving down and Landis called me and said, 'Come on down, I'm gonna be there, we'll sit in the back of the theater.' So my wife and I were looking for the theater in Westwood and we turned a corner and there was a line around the block. I thought that couldn't be our theater 'cause nobody knows about the movie yet. But it was. It was the line for *Animal House*. That night, I was pissed off when I saw the movie because the audience was laughing so loud—*screaming* with laughter—that you were missing some of the funny lines that were coming up. I remember saying to John, 'Oh my God! They didn't hear me say that line.' It was an amazing experience."

Kevin Bacon also remembers the night of the world premiere. "I got an invitation and I took the subway to the Astor in Times Square, but I got in line to go in, never having been to a premiere before. I'm standing in line watching all the limos pull up and, suddenly, there's Peter Riegert and Stephen Furst and Stephen sees me and yells, 'Kevin! What are you doing in line?' So, I joined them but my hair was long and after the movie nobody in the audience recognized me."

Film editor George Folsey was in London the night *Animal House* opened. He had only shortly before finished editing our film and supervising the making of the prints and other elements of the postproduction. To take a break, he and his wife had flown to visit friends in London. A few days after the opening, at three o'clock in the morning, London time, his phone rang. Both he and his wife startled awake. They had kids back in LA and when you get a 3 A.M. call, and you're six thousand miles away from your kids, you panic. He grabbed the phone and settled down when he realized it was John Landis calling. John went on and on about the opening-night screening, the opening-night party, and more important, the crowds trying to get in to see the movie. "It's a phenomenon," he yelled over the phone. He was so happy that Folsey had trouble understanding much of what he had to say, but he told him the studio was thrilled, and that Ivan and I were slapping backs, and shaking hands, and smiling a lot. George Folsey had never doubted that the movie was going to be successful, but perhaps not as successful as it was.

Mark Metcalf tells us that on opening night and in the days that followed he tended to hang around the theaters playing the movie, and guesses that he must have walked nearly a dozen "twelve-year-olds" into see the R-rated film.

Martha Smith saw the film at a cast-and-crew screening a few days before the opening. "I was pretty much traumatized by seeing myself that large on the screen. It seemed like I was fifteen times the size of myself up on the screen and I felt like running to the bathroom and getting sick."

"A week or so after the opening, when the picture had been screened in Denver," Peter Riegert recalls, "I called Landis and asked him how it went. He started making strange sounds. 'Ca-ching. Ca-ching.' I asked him what that meant. 'That,' he said, 'is the sound of a cash register.'

"Bette Midler and I went to the premiere together but had left for a weekend in the country before opening night.

When we returned to New York, we walked over to the Sutton to see if anybody was at *Animal House*. I got about twenty-five yards—less, twenty-five feet—from the entrance and there were four young guys that worked for the Sutton on a break having a cigarette and yakking on the corner. They saw me coming and all four of them together yelled 'Boone!' And I looked at Bette and I went 'Holy shit! They know the character's name?' And we walked in right before the horse got killed. It was in the middle of the movie and the theater's packed—it was bedlam. Now I knew what John meant by 'Ca-ching.'"

Karen Allen and John and Judy Belushi were at O'Lunney's Old Country Bar on Manhattan's East Side on opening night. John was too nervous to go to the theaters. At one point Karen got up and sang a song. John just sat quietly. He had asked a friend to check out the theaters and he was waiting for him to return. At one point, a customer came into the club and sat down near the table where Karen and the Belushis were. The man turned to John and said, "I just came from your movie." John sat up, "Did you like it?" he asked. "I don't know," he replied. "It was so crowded I couldn't get in."

John bought a round of drinks for the man's table.

That Monday morning, Walter Garibaldi came into my office with some of the calculations he'd made. He no longer needed the figures he'd computed with his calculator at the Sutton on opening night, since the industry's auditing system had already released early weekend box office results.

He had taken the new figures and sliced off what was then our five percent of the gross. Calculating a reasonable run of at least four or five weeks, he showed me an impressive figure. Our gross, however, quickly escalated to 17.5 percent and the movie ran for months. That eventually brought our share to tens of millions. Walter calculated only the domestic theatrical income. He did not include foreign sales, television sales, cable sales, and what later became most important, video and DVD sales. I looked at his figures and nodded. When he left, I sat and stared at my *Lampoon* colleagues. I guess, I mused, movies are where we're going.

The picture would eventually gross $140 million at theaters in the United States and Canada. Using today's ticket prices, its domestic box office gross would have exceeded $500 million. It was R-rated and few R movies reach these heights.

Then there were the reviews. Critics weren't known for pulling their punches. My favorite story about criticism of a play or movie is about Pia Zadora, a singer/actress whose career was financed by her wealthy husband. Probably apocryphal, the story tells of her playing the lead in the play *The Diary of Anne Frank*. In the scene where the Nazis break into the house that Anne Frank has been hiding in, someone in the audience yelled, "She's in the attic!"

One critic said of another play, "I saw this at a distinct disadvantage. The seats were facing the stage."

That said, *National Lampoon's Animal House* got great reviews but it also had its share of detractors. One word that was used in almost every review was "tasteless." Most said things like, "Tasteless but hilarious," or "Tasteless but you gotta see it!" A few just said "Tasteless," and went downhill from there.

On the morning of July 27, more reviews started coming

in. I sat on the floor of my office with four or five *Lampoon* staffers. There were newspapers all around the room. We had read the morning-paper reviews the previous evening, now we were reading the New York afternoon papers. Each one of us would read a different review. The phones rang persistently. Early that morning, LA time, Charlie Powell called from Universal. Charlie, of course, had uttered the amazing oath "I swear on my son's life that you have a major hit" just a few weeks before. I picked up the phone and said, "Good news, Charlie, the kid lives."

Staffers would walk by my office and poke their heads in. O'Rourke looked in, smiled, turned, and walked away. Ted Mann walked into the room and shrugged and said, "What's all the fuss about?" Then he turned, waved, and walked out.

Jeffrey Richards, our New York publicist, who some years later would go on to become a successful Broadway producer, sprinted into the room carrying more papers. It was like after the opening night of *Lemmings*, reading the reviews, only this time they were from New York, LA, Toronto, and Chicago.

On the Thursday night before Friday's opening, I had waited at a 59th Street newsstand for the early editions of the next day's newspapers. The first review of the movie I read was by Janet Maslin of *The New York Times*. This is, in part, what she wrote:

> *Animal House* is too cheerfully sleazy to be termed
> tame, but the filmmakers have been smart enough to
> leaven each gross-out with an element of innocent
> fun. Even the action-packed finale amounts to noth-

ing more dangerous than the spectacle of all heck breaking loose.

The filmmakers have simply supplied the appropriate panty girdles, crewneck sweaters, frat-house initiation rites and rituals of the toga party, and let all the idiocy speak—very eloquently, and with a lot of comic fervor—for itself.

On Friday, in Chicago, *Lampoon* editor John Hughes picked up a copy of the *Sun-Times* and read Roger Ebert's review to me.

The movie is vulgar, raunchy, ribald, and occasionally scatological. It is also the funniest comedy since Mel Brooks made *The Producers*. *Animal House* is funny for some of the same reasons the *National Lampoon* is funny (and Second City and *Saturday Night Live* are fun): because it finds some kind of precarious balance between insanity and accuracy, between cheerfully wretched excess and an ability to reproduce the most revealing nuances of human behavior.

In Boston, the film critic at the *Boston Metro* wrote:

The *National Lampoon* magazine, long a paragon of brilliant bad taste, was perhaps the perfect agent to immortalize the "animal fraternity." *National Lampoon's Animal House* is enjoyable for its own deliciously vulgar jokes and pranks, and of its resurrection of

1962, when the '50s actually reached its finest flower-
ing. The American college campus in 1962 was, by its
appearance in the movie at least, a bizarre place indeed.

The Cincinnati Post may have summed up how most reacted in its first sentence: "The summer of '78 may go into the
record books as the season when comedy came back to the
movies."

This was the headline in *The Miami Herald*: "*Animal
House:* Tons of Laughs." It continued:

Those thrilling days of yesteryear on the fraternity
front are raunchily relived in a new film from the
National Lampoon folks. Ramis, Kenney, and Miller
would have us acknowledge that the "animal house"
was the only true home of the brotherhood, but that's
really beside the point. The point is how funny they
can make the struggle between Faber's Delta Tau Chi
house and the forces of good—the dean, the cheer-
leaders, ROTC and the rival fraternity, suave Omega
House.

The *Pittsburgh Post-Gazette* started by comparing it to
the magazine:

It's difficult to describe the *National Lampoon* to someone who's never read it. Raw, biting, silly, hedonistic,
obscene, often hilarious and always amusing, its ma-

jor flaw is its almost exclusively male point of view. This is an apt description of *National Lampoon's Animal House*. Adapted from earlier material in the magazine, it has all the anarchy and lack of taste that has charmed so many of us.

The Cleveland's *Plain Dealer* explained: "Probably what makes *Animal House* so appealing is that buried in the ribald dialogue and lewdness there are good spirits and an understanding of the inconsistencies of college life."

The *Detroit Free Press*: "Raucous laughter fills *Animal House*," and goes on to say, "At last the great summer movie we've been waiting for."

The Dallas Morning News said, "*Animal House* offers unbridled humor," and, like just about everyone else, singled out Belushi.

And in the same state, the *Houston Chronicle* headlined: "Laughs Galore in *Animal House*." The review goes on to say: "This movie, face it, is a laugh riot. No other way to describe it."

The *Philadelphia Evening Bulletin* took an interesting look at it: "'Knowledge is good,' reads the inscription on the statue of the founder of Faber College. To the animals that inhabit Delta House, the lowliest fraternity on campus, the only relation between the words "knowledge" and "college" is that they rhyme."

The *Boston Phoenix* loved Belushi: "When John Belushi sprays mashed potatoes out of his mouth, yelling 'I'm a zit!' *National Lampoon's Animal House* is everything the nasty little kid in us could ever want. Humor like this is childish, witless, and revolting and that's exactly why we love it."

In the *Pittsburgh Post-Gazette*, a few weeks after the film opened, columnist Mike Kalina interviewed Jamie Widdoes. He asked him what his family's reaction to the movie was.

"My mother thought it was very 'male,'" he told him, "but my father thought it was hilarious. My grandmother [pause], well, I won't go into that reaction. But as a whole, my family certainly thought I was very good."

I had invited my own mother to see the movie. I told her I'd pick her and her friends up and take them to the theater. She told me she'd think about it. I kept calling her about it and she kept thinking about it. She never saw the movie.

Years earlier, before *Animal House*, a fan sent Michael O'Donoghue a package at the *Lampoon*. The mailroom clerk told me it was ticking. I checked it out and immediately called the police. The bomb squad cleared out the building and Madison Avenue from 56th Street to 62nd Street. The building was empty but I sneaked up to a top floor that housed our recording studio and began calling the newspapers: Once a press agent, always a press agent. If we were going to get a bomb, I wanted press coverage. I suddenly remembered that my mother spent most of her day listening to the radio, so I called her and told her not to worry, that the police had everything under control. "Sure," she responded. "You get a bomb. That's because you publish that dirty magazine."

O'Donoghue's bomb was real. We were to get bombs of another kind from a handful of critics.

It struck me that a few of the movie critics felt the same way about the movie as my mother did about the magazine.

Pat Collins in the New York's *Daily News* simply hated the movie. Like most critics she thought it was "tasteless," but unlike most critics, she didn't think it was funny.

The *St. Louis Globe-Democrat* called the movie a "comedic near miss." It's described in the review as "the sort of thing the *National Lampoon* should satirize, not lend its name to."

Leonard Maltin, a critic who frequently appears on TV and writes a book of film reviews updated each year gave *Animal House* two out of four stars, calling it only "sporadically funny."

A critic who reviewed the film in *The Boston Globe* didn't think it was funny—didn't like it at all. Six months later he wrote, "Because of the great popularity, I've seen it twice since, [and] I still don't like it," apparently unwilling to suggest that maybe he was just having a bad day. But, he went on to comment, "I must admit there are hilarious scenes in the film. . . . When John Belushi peers through the window of the sorority house and gives a conspiratorial wink to the audience, it's funny. He speaks to those repressed tendencies that aren't allowed to exist in our allegedly nonsexist collective consciousness."

He ended by quoting what screenwriter Chris Miller had once said to him during an interview: "The theme of the movie is that *fun* is good." "Maybe so," the writer ended with, "but *Animal House* isn't."

Syndicated film critic Rex Reed didn't like it either.

National Lampoon's Animal House is a comic book on film. It has the infamous, irreverent attitude the *Lampoon* is noted for but it lacks the substance and style to make it truly satisfying. For all of its high-spirited fun and clever skits, it's rather like watching paint drying. The parody goes lame with the jokes that start out fresh and go from stale to limp, like potato chips left out overnight.

A review in the *North Shore Weeklies* in Massachusetts was headlined in no uncertain terms: *"Animal House* Devoid of Humor."

The *Wilmington Sunday News Journal* reviewed the film as follows:

The group of young actors do the best they can with the script and situations and there is an occasional hint that director John Landis may actually have been on the set. For reasons best known to Donald Sutherland, he is also in the film.

The makers of this film might have done well to watch some Keaton films, the Pink Panther series, and a lot of others to learn what makes good comedy. They have certainly missed the mark with *Animal House.*

Somehow one would suspect they didn't think much of it.

Comedian Larry Miller nicely summed up what the comedy community thought of the film: "Anyone who doesn't think it's funny," he said gently, "should be executed."

A week after the movie opened all across the United States and Canada we carefully calculated 110 newspaper reviews and came up with 86 "hilarious," 10 in which the critic liked parts, didn't like other parts and 14 that didn't like any parts.

Not all the attention was given solely to the film. As usual, the stars of the movie, the producers, and the director were doing interviews on television and radio and for newspapers and magazines across the country. As with Jamie Widdoes, every hometown of every actor that had at least one line in the movie was carrying stories on them. In a second wave of publicity, newspapers and magazines everywhere started writing about the new craze inspired by the movie: toga parties.

Across a full-page banner headline, the prestigious *Washington Post* screamed, "Toga! Toga! Toga!" Below it ran a three-column-wide picture of dozens of young college students dressed in togas and waving widely, with a subhead that read, "Inspired by *National Lampoon's Animal House*: The toga party, this semester's ritual of college exhibitionism is cropping up at campuses across the country!" They then went on to a half-page story that began: "'The theme of the party,' said a young man wearing a tinfoil helmet and toga, 'was to get orgiastic.' And the required dress for the evening was 'dress' togas."

At colleges everywhere, students were not just wearing bedsheets, they were wearing decorated togas, colored togas with ribbons and beads and spangles and drawings, togas with long sleeves and short sleeves and no sleeves. Headbands with Greek lettering were in style as were those similar to Belushi's laurel crown. Coming up with a new toga design was the thing to do.

At first, we staged a couple of toga parties ourselves, in the name of publicity. We had one at University of Southern California, attended by 20,000 college students in togas, and then, naturally, one at the University of Oregon, where thousands came to drink beer and dance to "Shout!" But soon after we didn't have to stage them at all. Colleges everywhere were starting to have their own toga parties. The University of Wisconsin had one that attracted more than 30,000 students in sheets and togas. NYU, University of Michigan, University of Iowa, San Diego State, University of North Dakota, University of Maine, and even the university where it all started, Harvard, joined in, followed by another at Yale. And all these parties occurred within days after the movie opened in late July. It seemed like *Animal House* was everywhere. You read about it, heard about it, talked about it, and danced to it.

A month or so after it opened I remember visiting one of my sons at Kenyon College in Gambier, Ohio. When I walked up to the dorm I saw a poster on the dorm door. It was the movie poster with caricatures of all the Deltas standing in front of their house. Next to each caricature was the name of one of my son's fellow students: One would be Bluto, one would be Otter, another D-Day, and so on. Obviously, the crazy guy in his dorm would be Bluto; the lover, Otter.

They didn't do that because I was coming to visit, they did it because they were college students and *they could do anything they wanted to do.* And at that moment, at that time of their lives, Bluto, Otter, and the gang were who they wanted to be.

When *Newsweek* ran a cover with Belushi in a toga, the movie had already become a runaway hit. The magazine heralded the movie as "the beginning of the new college humor."

Doug Kenney would say: "First this was a Doug Kenney, Harold Ramis movie; then a Doug Kenney, Harold Ramis, and Chris Miller movie; then a Matty Simmons and Ivan Reitman movie; then a John Landis movie. And now it's a John Belushi movie."

16

CUTS, OUTTAKES, AND SEQUELS

A scene that never made it to the final film was inspired by "The Night of the Seven Fires," one of Chris Miller's short stories that the theme of the script was based on. The story describes in detail how Delta pledges had to march up the side of a mountain and continually drink beer until they could vomit into each of seven fires that lit up along the mountain. I hated scatological humor and still do. I insisted they take out all the throwing up, pissing, and shitting.

If you recall the scene when the Deltas are called into Dean Wormer's office, they had all been drunk the night before, especially Flounder, who quite obviously couldn't hold his liquor. When Dean Wormer tells them they're going to be kicked out of school, Flounder throws up on the dean. The way it was written, he would actually throw up on camera. "No," I insisted. "When it looks like he's about to vomit we cut to the outer office where the quirky secretary sits and we *hear* Flounder throwing up." Eventually everyone agreed that it would be funnier for the audience to use their imagination rather than see such a violent upsurge.

My favorite scene that was taken out of the script before filming was when the Deltas go on their road trip. They're speeding along in Flounder's brother's car when suddenly they pass a scraggly musician, guitar slung over his shoulder, cowboy hat on his head, and a weary look on his face, as he thumbs for a ride. The Delta car screeches to a halt, a door flies open, and the traveler gets in. We cut to the interior of the car and Otter starts a conversation with the young man.

"You're a musician?"

"Yep, singer, songwriter, musician."

"What's your name?"

"Zimmerman," says the musician in a recognizable twangy voice.

"Well, Zimmerman, play something for us."

We cut back to the outside of the car and we hear that familiar Bob Dylan nasal singing. This goes on for a few beats, the car again comes to a screeching halt, the door flies open once more, and Zimmerman—or Dylan, if you prefer—is tossed out onto the road.

I always loved that scene. I'd planned to ask Chris Guest, who'd done a Dylan impersonation in *Lemmings*, to play the part but we finally decided that it would extend the road trip scene too long and that the really hilarious parts were the pickup at the girls' college and the scene in the bar.

John Landis has always insisted that *National Lampoon's Animal House* was "a sweet movie." Well, that didn't exactly match the reviews or the reaction of the public, who thought it was raucous and explosive. He remains, to this day, the only one who used the word "sweet" in describing it. But maybe he was right, at least about some of it. What follows is a scene that *was* sweet but was cut from the script early on.

In this scene we meet Clorette, the teenage daughter of the town mayor, who almost becomes "Pinto's first lay." In the excerpt below, Pinto and Flounder are called Kent and Larry, respectively, because they have not yet earned their Delta names. Clorette is a customer at a pizza parlor in this version (in the film, when we meet her she's working at the checkout counter at a supermarket). Flounder believes the Deltas didn't like him and he doesn't think he's going to be invited to join the fraternity.

INT. SHAKEY'S PIZZA – NIGHT

Kent has a large pizza in front of him with a slice in each hand. Larry is sipping a coke.

> **KENT (dismal)**
> I bet they won't even take me.

Larry is preoccupied, gazing at three local teenage girls as they come walking into Shakey's.

> **LARRY (absently)**
> I thought you said they had to take you 'cause your brother was a member.

KENT

Yeah, but I make a lousy first impression.

LARRY

Who told you that?

KENT

My mother. (He bites into his pizza.)

Larry continues to stare at the three teenage girls as they carry their pizza to a table. One of the girls, a cute little brunette, crosses to Larry and Kent's table. Larry strikes a casual pose. Later we'll learn that this girl's name is CLORETTE.

CLORETTE (chewing gum)

Either of you guys 21? That creep won't sell us a beer.

Larry and Kent answer simultaneously.

LARRY

Yes.

KENT

No.

LARRY (covering)

I am, he's not. But I left my wallet in my room.
All my ID's are in it.

Kent rolls his eyes and chortles through a mouthful of pizza.

CLORETTE
Thanks anyway. Maybe some other time.

KENT
Yeah, in about three years.

Clorette walks away. Larry turns and gives Kent a hard noogie punch on the shoulder.

As editor George Folsey said, more than a half hour was deleted from the first rough cut of the script to get the running time down to what it was when the film was released. Folsey remembers one of the scenes that was cut was after the Deltas leave the Dexter Lake Club. "We cut back to the girls who are now playing pool with the black guys they met at the bar, and nobody knows what to do. They're all really uncomfortable and nervous, but the humor in the scene was that the black guys are more uncomfortable in this situation than the white girls are. So there are lines thrown around like, one guy says, 'I have to go home and see my mother,' and another guy says, 'I think I left the water running in my bathtub.' They say anything to get out of there so they don't have to deal with these girls."

When we cut that scene there was no resolution to what happened to the girls after the Deltas left the club. I insisted that there had to be something to show what happened to the girls, thus a scene was shot with the girls walking back to their school complaining about how rude the boys were, except for the one girl who was in the car with Otter. She murmurs, "I don't know. I think Otter was pretty cute."

There were other scenes left on the cutting room floor:

Pinto taken to a whorehouse for his "first lay." Cut.
Football game between the Omegas and Deltas. Cut.
More anger from Katy toward Boone about his life-style. Cut and softened.
Flounder finally getting mad at Otter and Boone and fellow Deltas. Cut and softened.

Also cut were many lines from Bluto. Everybody agreed that the Bluto character should do little talking and a lot of physical humor. Belushi, of course, could do anything, but in physical comedy he was unmatched. We figured there was enough conversation in the picture and Bluto was the action figure. Cut, cut, cut, cut.

And then there was the scene in which Mandy is speaking to a group of younger female students. Suddenly, D-Day appears, blood pouring from his hands and face. The girls immediately realize that he's clowning and it's fake blood, but Bluto leaps into the scene, turns to the girls, and shouts, "It's okay, ladies, I'm a doctor. Now, all of you take off your underpants and cut them into little strips so I can administer to this man!" The girls stalk off in disgust. Cut.

Eventually, we felt that Otter should be the womanizer and fast-talker of the group, whereas in the first draft of the script, Boone was the Delta who went into the girl's sorority house to ask for Fawn Lebowitz. The switch worked.

A scene implying that Otter has just had sex with Sissy, Flounder's girlfriend. Cut. This scene, cut from an early script, takes place at the first Delta House party. Otter puts an arm around Sissy's shoulder and they disappear. Later, Flounder sees them coming out of Otter's room, as Otter is stuffing his shirt back in his pants and Sissy is straightening her panties. Because the audience wouldn't like Otter doing that to a sweet guy like Flounder, we felt the scene would not suit our heroes.

There was also a character named Einswine, who was cut from the film altogether, but later revived for the TV show that would follow, *Delta House.* Einswine was the school genius who had a steady business of supplying term papers, test answers—whatever the students needed. The character appeared in the January 1977 draft of the script.

Boone takes Pinto to see Einswine about an economics paper he hadn't written and had no idea how to write. Very businesslike, Einswine asks Pinto what sort of grade he would like. Pinto settles for a B and Einswine sells him a term paper. Later, Pinto is called into the office of the economics professor, who asks him if he's ever heard of Arnold Toynbee. Pinto asks him if that's the kid who sits next to him in class. The professor tells Pinto that Toynbee was one of the world's great economists and that his term paper was an exact duplicate of something Toynbee had written before he died in 1936. Innocently, Pinto replies, "Oh, well, then he died before I was born."

"Good." says the professor. "Then we know he didn't copy the paper from you."

Animal House was made into a TV show, but no feature-film sequels to *Animal House* have ever been made. In between arguments from those studio heads who felt there shouldn't be a sequel, there were a couple who thought we should give it a try. Three were written.

One who was in favor was Ned Tanen, three years after *Animal House* came out. The original writers of the screenplay had gone on to their own projects and passed on writing a sequel. So I came up with a trio of *Lampoon* writers and editors: John Weidman and Tim Crouse, and then *Lampoon* editor, John Hughes.

They brought back the football game that had been cut from our original script and once again it didn't work. In their story the year is established as 1966. The Omegas and Deltas have graduated or, as we learned in the original movie, been thrown out of school. At first we meet Doug Niedermeyer and his younger brother, Brad, who is now the Omega leader. The rumor that Doug had been killed in Vietnam was obviously untrue.

Bluto was again a central character in this first sequel. The traits and characteristics of all of the principals of the first movie were kept intact. Otter is still a womanizer. Boone is still a music lover who has since divorced Katy. Flounder is fatter than ever and eats continuously. D-Day is, well, D-Day. And Hoover is still insecure. We don't meet Pinto until late in the script, when we discover he has become a successful corporate raider and a huge contributor to the school.

The script simply wasn't right. Perhaps it was too soon and the characters in the first picture too familiar to try a sequel. Whatever the reason, we all agreed that it didn't work.

There were some very well written scenes and some good ideas, though. The new characters were mostly young Omegas and Deltas. One of the most interesting of the new women introduced in this sequel was Naomi, a pretty airhead, and obviously someone who enjoyed sex. She becomes "Flounder's first lay."

In one scene, they are in the bushes near a party they've attended. They are disrobing, she with practiced ease and he with clumsy anxiety. She tells him about her past:

NAOMI

I went with a guy who shot methadone for a while, but I never got any sleep. Then I lived with a rock star who ate psychedelic mushrooms for breakfast, which is gastronomically incorrect 'cause everyone knows you should have grains for breakfast, and then I had a couple of dudes who were into reds. But I think self-help is the wave of the future.

She smiles lasciviously.

I've always wanted to get it on with a guy who was into straight encounter stuff.

[She drops her dress, revealing a naked and amazing body.]

FLOUNDER (Eyes bulging.)

Oh, boy. Is this great!

In 1995, Casey Silver, then president of Universal, gave us the go-ahead to once again develop a sequel. Ivan Reitman and I disagreed on the storyline. He wanted it to be primarily about the new students some years later, and not bring in the old Deltas until we are well into the third act of the screenplay. I urged that we bring the Deltas in almost immediately. I felt that the public wanted to see the Deltas, even if they were older. Viewers would want to know what they were doing after they were kicked out of Faber. The studio agreed with Ivan, and screenwriter John Fasano wrote the screenplay. That didn't work either.

In Fasano's screenplay, John Blutarsky Jr., son of the late Bluto, is now a Delta. He contacts all the older Deltas and tells them he needs their help, that there's an emergency. They arrive to discover that the Deltas are now being totally repressed by Wormer. Junior wants to strike back.

OTTER (Otter is indignant and in disbelief.)

Wait just a damn minute. Do you mean that you made us fly from all over the country—leave our jobs, our businesses, our careers, our families, my incredibly beautiful patients missing their gynocologist—Boone came all the way from Australia, just for a fraternity prank? You disrupted all our lives just to help you fuck Dean Wormer?

JUNIOR
Yes.

OTTER (nods approvingly)
I buy that.

A year later, Casey asked me to write the script my way.

In my script we meet Otter and Boone in 1982, twenty years after they left Faber. Boone now owns a taxi cab company in Boston and Otter is a successful gynecologist. They run into each other when they attend conventions for their respective industries being held in the same hotel, and they sit and drink and talk and reminisce about their college days. Both say they haven't been happy since they left Faber. Otter tells Boone that he read in a copy of the alumni newspaper and that Wormer is retiring. In a week or so they're having an honorary gathering for him at which they will unveil a statue of him, to be erected right next to that of Emil Faber. Both men are infuriated and they decide that they should round up their Delta crew and once again raise hell at Faber, the destruction of Wormer's statue their particular target.

They've met two women at the convention hotel, one of whom owns a chain of limos. The four of them embark on a limo caravan ("Road trip!") and pick up their former Delta mates while en route to Faber.

All of them have changed. Some of them are married with kids, and are henpecked—including, astonishingly enough,

D-Day, who also has a steady job and a hefty mortgage. Flounder is divorced and living with his brother who treats him terribly.

On the way to Faber, they hear that Bluto has died, apparently of a heart attack in the lavatory of an airplane; it is noted that the stewardess survived.

One of the women from the convention tells Otter she thinks his whole "mission" to return to Faber is ridiculous. "Holding a grudge after twenty years . . . it's . . . it's childish," she says. He answers:

> This is more than a grudge. Actually, I don't even hate Wormer. It's more like the biggest game of my life— like the World Series or the Super Bowl. The Deltas against the Wormers. And now there's even more involved. It's for Bluto. Anarchy in Bluto's name. Having fun is something people do when they're not working or studying or raising kids. Not Bluto. Having fun was a way of life for him and he had a kind of unique theory of what having fun constituted. I guess we all did but Bluto set the style and pace. This plan, getting back at Wormer, after all these years? Boone and I may have come up with it but it was a Bluto idea.

The Deltas, older, more settled, and with not nearly as much energy, nevertheless conquer once again, and the Wormer celebration is totally disrupted and the statue destroyed.

Universal decided not to proceed with a sequel and I haven't brought it up again.

17

ANIMAL HOUSE, THE NEXT DECADE

The late character actor Edmund Gwenn, best known for his portrayal of Santa Claus in the original *Miracle on 34th Street*, spent the last years of his life at the Actor's Home in Southern California. Supposedly, when he was dying, a friend came to visit him and tried to console him. "I'm so sorry, Edmund. It must be tough." Gwenn looked up and answered slowly, "Dying is easy. Comedy is tough."

Hollywood is a tough place, and comedy is even tougher. In the film business, the highs are incredibly high and the lows are dismally low. The biggest stars are on top of the world when they have a hit and fall into some bottomless pit when the movie they're in flops. In 1978 and 1979, after *Animal House*, all of us who were involved with the picture were on tremendous highs. I made a deal with Universal and they gave me the biggest producer's office on the lot, with full staff, expenses, and a research and development department. At lunch in the commissary, Lew Wasserman, the most powerful man in the industry, would walk by my table, put a hand on my shoulder and ask, "How's my partner today?" I bought a house in Beverly Hills and every Sunday night my wife and I went to Chasen's for what was then the industry's legendary Sunday night dinner. Because I was temporarily a hot Hollywood producer, I was seated in the outer room where big stars and temporarily hot producers sat. At a nearby table would be Cary Grant or Jimmy Stewart. Perhaps across the room would be Ronald Reagan, soon to be president, or Frank Sinatra. I would tell my friends back East that I was the only one in the room I didn't recognize.

Then I had to go back to work at the *Lampoon*. I would fly back and forth between New York and LA. In New York the circulation of the magazine was at an all-time high of 1.2 million, in part because of the movie. At Universal, my next-door neighbors were Richard Zanuck and David Brown, who had produced, among many hits, *Jaws* and *The Sting*. One afternoon I bumped into David and we agreed to have lunch together in New York a few days later. Over lunch he said to me, "Dick and I would love to make a movie with you."

Without really thinking, I shot back at him, "*National Lampoon's Jaws 3, People 0.*" He looked up, not knowing whether to laugh or shake my hand. I then proceeded to tell a story that I made up as I went along, about the making of *Jaws 3*. The running gag in the story would be that the director, a would-be Spielberg, is constantly attacked by the shark and has parts of his anatomy bitten off in different scenes, winding up without a foot, several fingers, and so forth. David broke out laughing.

"I love it," he said. "Let's do it! You produce it. Dick and I will be executive producers." He got up. "I gotta call Dick," and he ran to the phone. Minutes later he was back. "Dick loves it too," he said, "and we're meeting Ned Tanen at the Rainbow Grill tonight. I'll call you in the morning. We want to do it."

After lunch, I literally ran back to my office, called in my assistant Barbara Atti, and dictated the story that I had just made up. The next morning David phoned me. "Tanen loved it," he said. You pick the writers and have your lawyer call Business Affairs at Universal and make a deal."

I was delighted and walked back into the editorial offices. John Hughes was sitting at a desk talking to Tod Carroll, another *Lampoon* editor. I beckoned them to come to my office. I handed them the story outline I had written. "You're going to write the screenplay for this," I said. "Universal is going to make it and I'm producing it with Zanuck and Brown." John Hughes, who had not yet written a screenplay, but was normally laid back and utterly cool, shook his head in disbelief. Carroll was speechless. We had a movie.

Meanwhile, Sid Sheinberg had other ideas. I met him in his office one afternoon in 1979 and he told me he wanted to bring *Animal House* to television. I told him about *Jaws 3* and he said I could do both. I was hesitant. I wanted to wait a couple of years and do an *Animal House* sequel. Sheinberg was TV oriented at that time. Television was where they were making big money with syndication and he thought *Animal House* would be a surefire hit. I told him that I was concerned that television wouldn't give us the latitude that we had in film and that it would be too tame. We met many times and finally, and reluctantly, I agreed to do it.

Doug Kenney, Harold Ramis, and Chris Miller agreed to write the first episode of *Delta House,* the name we had given the new *Animal House* TV series. What we discovered after agreeing to make the deal with Universal and ABC was that both CBS and NBC would have college fraternity TV shows debut the same week as ours.

I tried to get all the original Deltas for the TV show but Belushi was now a star and he passed, and Matheson was on the verge of becoming a star and didn't want to do a television series. Nor did Karen Allen, Peter Riegert, Kevin Bacon, or Tom Hulce. John Vernon, Bruce McGill, Jamie Widdoes, and Stephen Furst agreed to reprise their roles. We began work on the first episode and it was then that I learned for the first time that ABC had planned to put *Delta House* on at eight o'clock.

Back in 1979, the eight-to-nine time slot on network television was called the "Family Hour" and it was aimed strictly at families with small children. My earlier fears of censorship became a nightmare. I was told my characters couldn't drink beer; a girl and a boy couldn't sit, fully clothed, on a bed together—and in tiny dorm rooms the bed is often the only place you can sit. There were many other rules: Certainly the language had to be doctored, even if the words weren't obscene but merely suggestive. I yelled and argued. The heads of comedy in Los Angeles for NBC were Marcy Carsey and Tom Werner, who would later go on to great success with such sitcoms as *Friends* and *The Bill Cosby Show,* but they insisted that they didn't have the power to move our time slot and that "New York made those decisions." I tried to meet with "New York," but they didn't want to discuss it. Finally, we went on the air the same week the other two network frat shows premiered. They got terrible reviews and one was cancelled shortly after it began to air. We got good reviews but the ratings weren't nearly as high as we had anticipated and I was still furious over the hour they had put us in and the resultant censorship. Their ten o'clock time slots were taken mostly by hour-long dramas, but I pleaded for at least a nine-thirty slot where we could do our kind of comedy. After all, this was *Animal House*. After three shows they moved us to nine-thirty. Our ratings soared and we were the number-one show for that time slot. Two weeks later they moved us back to eight. I gave ABC an ultimatum: "Put us on later in the evening or we're not going to continue."

Contractually, I had no right to make such a demand but everybody in the cast was with me. Once again, ABC moved us back to the nine-thirty slot, and once again, a week later, they moved us back to eight. Audiences never knew when we would be on until the day of airing. I told them again that this would not work out.

We started having internal problems. Many of our top writers were discouraged by the censorship.

Hughes and I wrote a number of the early episodes. There were also scripts by Al Jean and Michael Reiss, and other *Lampoon* writers and editors. They, and others, would be put off by the network's censorship and ease away from the project.

A new character to be added to *Delta House* was named

only "the Bombshell." We wanted a totally unknown girl. She had to be sexy and incredibly beautiful and, hopefully, be able to act at least a little. Agents kept sending us actresses but none of them were right. Finally, we issued a "cattle call." This is when actors, primarily unknowns, come and stand in long lines waiting for the chance to audition. If a particular actor on line looked good they would read for the role. We went through 938 (by actual count) actresses who were looking to be "the Bombshell." They were either not beautiful or sexy enough or couldn't act well enough. Finally, a girl walked into the room and I said to our casting director, "If this girl can talk, she's got the part." She was truly one of the most exciting young women I had ever seen. We had her read and she did well although she had never acted professionally.

After the casting call I called Marcy Carsey and told her I'd gotten the girl for the Bombshell role. "If she hasn't acted professionally before," Marcy said, "you're going to have to give her a screen test."

I argued, insisting that the girl could act well enough and was just perfect for such a name, for such a role." Marcy persisted and we arranged for a screen test. I directed it and when I looked through the lens I could see that the camera admired her as much as I did.

When I told her that she got the part, she smiled and asked, "What do I do about my job? I work the checkout counter at Von's supermarket in Orange County."

"Well," I said. "You're out of the grocery business forever."

Michelle Pfeiffer became the Bombshell.

Doug Kenney (Stork) suddenly leads the disastrous Homecoming Parade.

The Deltas huddle offscreen around Verna Bloom (Mrs. Wormer).

Three of the film's villains before the parade: Cesare Danova (Mayor Carmine DePasto), John Vernon (Dean Wormer), and James Daughton (Greg Marmalard).

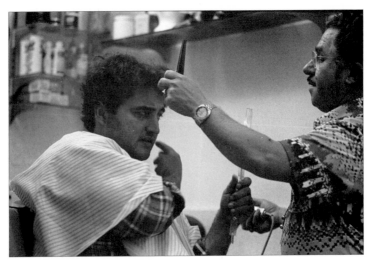

Belushi: "More off the sides — and get me a beer!"

The Deltas.

Simmons, Landis, and Belushi.

Otis Day and the Knights . . . "You make me wanna SHOUT!"

Director Landis setting up the opening scene with freshmen Tom Hulce (Larry Kroeger) and Stephen Furst (Kent Dorfman). They would later be Pinto and Flounder.

The Deltas and their house.

Kevin Bacon (Chip), Mark Metcalf (Niedermeyer), and their fellow Omegas. "Thank you, Sir, may I have another."

Peter Riegert in the only other quiet moment.

Tim Matheson and
Verna Bloom. Let the
games begin.

Screenwriters Doug Kenney and Chris Miller were indeed as nutty as the script suggests.

issue in 1980

THEY'RE LAMPOONING, if that's what you call attending the New York City premiere of "National Lampoon's Animal House," Bette Midler and a friend, Peter Riegert (left), showed up for the screening with actor Donald Sutherland, who appears in the comedy produced by the National Lampoon humor magazine.

Riegert and Sutherland with Bette Midler, Peter's girlfriend at the time.

The Washington Post

STYLE

Entertainment / The Arts / Leisure

TUESDAY, SEPTEMBER 26, 1978   C1

TOGA! TOGA! TOGA!

Inspired by the National Lampoon's "Animal House," the toga party, this semester's ritual of collegiate exhibitionism, is popping up at campuses across the country.

The country going toga crazy.

In the same office used by Dean Wormer in the film, University of Oregon President Richard Lariviere stands next to the "horse" that his staff gave him on his sixtieth birthday.

The show lasted one season. We simply could not write the kind of scripts we wanted to write with the restrictions ABC put on us. It was a mutual parting. In later years, Carsey and Werner's show *Friends* would basically be all about sex. Things changed at the networks.

By now Hughes and Carroll had finished the script for *Jaws 3, People 0*, and I hired a young director named Joe Dante, who a few years later would become an important filmmaker. We had a cast that included another young beauty, Bo Derek, whose first film *10* was due out shortly. I remember walking into the commissary with Bo: A room that was normally filled with conversation and plates and silverware clashing, people bouncing from table to table, suddenly became hushed. Every eye in the place turned to see this incredibly gorgeous young woman. When we sat down at the table I started to get notes from guys all over the room: "Matty, can I come over and say 'hello'?" or "Matty, what's her name?"

10 came out, Bo immediately became a star, and the studio got even more enthused by our picture. Our leading lady was to be literally half nude throughout a good portion of the film.

We spent most of a year preparing for the shoot. We had cast it and the studio had invested nearly $2 million building mechanical sharks. We had scouted locations and picked the Salton Sea in Southern California as ideal. We were ready to go.

Then the "down" of the "ups and downs" hit. Tanen called me and asked if he could see me. When I walked into his office I saw something I had never seen before in the business world, a tear was rolling down the side of his face. I had a small hunch then that I had a large problem. He told me immediately that he had to pull the plug on the movie. Dazed, I asked why, and he wouldn't give me an answer. I was furious. I went back to my office, called my lawyers, and immediately ended the three-year contract I had with Universal. When Zanuck and Brown were told about it, they broke their contract as well. We took with us what would become the *National Lampoon's Vacation* series, starting with *Vacation* in 1982, and in their case *Cocoon* and other pictures. We still couldn't get an explanation out of Tanen, nor could the press, who made a major story of this battle on the entertainment pages and in the trades.

Years later, Thom Mount told me that Steven Spielberg had gone to Sid Sheinberg and told him that if we made this movie that satirized his classic, and in his mind made fun of its director, he'd leave the studio. So, in the long run, the studio made a move they had to make. Spielberg was too valuable to lose. They lost Simmons, the *National Lampoon,* Zanuck and Brown, but kept Spielberg. If I had been them I would have made the same decision.

One of those dream-come-true Hollywood success stories almost happened during the preparation of *National Lampoon's Jaws 3, People 0.* About the same time *Animal House* came out, back in New York we started preparing a new musical revue to be called "That's Not Funny, That's Sick." We had a good cast and a good script. We were looking for an understudy. And, in the famous Broadway tradition, the understudy came running in to save the show and became a star overnight.

We had auditioned three or four different actors for the job. And finally we hired a guy who had come from Arkansas to New York to see if he could make it as an actor. At the time we hired him, he was going to bartender school. He had been passed on so many auditions he had just about given up hope. When he sang and acted for us, we hired him immediately. Just before the show opened, one of our leads, Lee Wilkoff, was offered the lead role in the off-Broadway production of *Little Shop of Horrors*. We had a contract but I let him out of it. And the understudy, Rodger Bumpass, took his place.

The show opened on the road and it traveled to some forty cities around the country. Wherever it went, Bumpass got great reviews. He was funny. He could sing. He moved smoothly and could dance, and had a magnificent speaking voice that he could use with either a deep baritone or a high falsetto.

After *Animal House* was released, the show had arrived to play the Roxy on Sunset Strip in Los Angeles. We were preparing *Jaws 3, People 0* and I invited Thom Mount and Sean Daniel to the opening of the show, especially to see Rodger. Like everyone else who saw the show, they thought he was terrific, and when I proposed he be the unknown star of the movie we were working on, they agreed with me, went to Tanen, and he approved.

So now, here was Rodger Bumpass, less than year out of Little Rock, Arkansas, and ready to star in a Universal Studios parody of *Jaws*, and his leading lady—by now, known all over the world—was Bo Derek. Rodger spent that summer working out, taking more acting lessons, and preparing for the role that would change his life.

Then, the picture was cancelled. Since then, Rodger has done a lot of television work, he's appeared in several plays and musicals (including the *Lampoon*'s "Class of '86"), and finally, after doing voice-overs for animated movies and TV shows for years, he became the voice of Squidward Tentacles in *SpongeBob SquarePants*, the hugely successful animated TV show. But Rodger has never starred in a feature film and should have.

Animal House continues through the years to be a movie you could see almost every day on television or cable. We weren't as fortunate with our next try, *National Lampoon's Movie Madness*. We put four stories together in one movie, parodies of such genres as the cop movie, the divorce movie, the making-it-big movie, and the terrorist movie. The cast included Peter Riegert, Robert Culp, Olympia Dukakis, Robby Benson, and Richard Widmark. It also included Diane Lane, a fourteen-year-old who had been very successful in her first picture, *A Little Romance*. Scenes between Peter and Diane in *Movie Madness* are possibly worth the price of admission but the rest of the movie didn't come off as well.

When John Hughes was on the *Lampoon* staff, he wrote a short story called "Vacation '63." It was loosely based on a cross-country trip he had taken with his parents and sister. When I read it, I told John that we would make a movie of it. I loved the story because I could relate to it, remembering when my father took us on long road trips or when I took my kids on similar drives. There were times that were wonderfully happy and others absolutely miserable.

John Ptak, my agent at William Morris, brought the script to Paramount, since I had left Universal. Jeff Katzenberg, then a vice-president at that studio, called to tell me that although it was a good script, it was "too sequential."

"I know it's sequential," I said. "It's about a family that goes from place to place all over the country. The goal was Walley World, or in John's original story, Disneyland. My argument didn't seem to impress Katzenberg, and he passed.

Then I had breakfast with Mark Canton, a vice-president at Warner Bros., who had become a hero at the studio because he had brought in and championed the Prince film *Purple Rain*. He hadn't read our script, only the short story in the magazine, but he wanted to do a movie with the *National Lampoon*. He was another *Animal House* devotee. His bosses at the studio read the first draft of the script that Hughes had written but didn't think much of it. This time the word they used was "episodic." I used the same argument that I had with Katzenberg, but it was really thanks to Canton's pushing and pleading that Warner Bros. went with the movie.

Immediately, we thought of Chevy Chase for Clark Griswold. We then auditioned four well-known actresses for the role of his long suffering wife, Ellen. The problem was that Harold Ramis, who would direct the picture, wanted one actress for the role, the casting director another, the studio a third, and I wanted number four, Beverly D'Angelo. The feeling among the others was that she might be a little young to have a fourteen- or fifteen-year-old child but I believed she could easily play the role, even though she was only thirty at the time.

Ramis came up with Randy Quaid for yokel Cousin Eddie, whom the Griswolds visit during their travels. I suggested Imogene Coca for cranky Aunt Edna, Eddie Bracken for the Walt Disney character, Roy Walley, and then Christie Brinkley as the beautiful blonde Chevy keeps seeing as they drive toward Walley World. The kids weren't that easy and we auditioned hundreds of them, finally selecting Dana Barron as Audrey and Anthony Michael Hall as Rusty. Both went on to long careers in film and television, with Michael, for a number of years, being a leading teen star.

So *Vacation*, since it was "sequential" and "episodic," was shot on the road, was released to great reviews, and made so much money that the studio beckoned and suggested a sequel. Eventually, we did four: *European Vacation*, *Christmas Vacation*, *Vegas Vacation*, and *Christmas Vacation 2* (the last, for television). The original *Christmas Vacation* remains the number-one Christmas movie of all time. It's seen more on television than any other holiday movie and has sold more videos.

In 1986, we produced another New York musical, *National Lampoon's Class of '86*. Among the actors who came from that show were John Michael Higgins, Veanne Cox (who was later to win a Tony on Broadway and play a villain in Julia Roberts's film *Erin Brockovich*), and Rodger Bumpass.

While all this was going on, people in the movie business were busy churning out college fraternity movies. There must have been fifty of them after *Animal House*. Every one had a mean dean and a "Bluto" character who would do so many of the things that the original did but not as well. Even *National Lampoon*'s *Van Wilder* had its mean dean, and the Van Wilder character was, essentially, a remake of Otter. The premise was that hapless college buddies were in a constant struggle with the bullies of the university—the same premise of all fifty of the frat movies that followed the original. I have watched films where entire passages of dialogue have been taken from *Animal House* and put into these new versions. Not just characters but lines and gags and stunts and scenes.

We filmed *Christmas Vacation* in 1989. It was an easy shoot, mostly on the Warner Bros. lot. The older relatives who came to visit the Griswolds were all new to the series but Chevy and Beverly were still there, along with Randy Quaid and Miriam Flynn, who played his wife in the original film. The actors who played Rusty and Audrey have always been different because of the time lapses between the sequels. We wanted to keep them as teenagers and by the time, for example, *Christmas Vacation* was shot, Anthony Michael Hall and Dana Barron were both in their twenties. Dana did, however, reprise the role in the TV movie *Christmas Vacation 2,* and Randy Quaid was the star of the movie. Chevy, at the time, didn't want to make a television movie and passed. The network came up with idea of rewriting it as a Cousin Eddie movie. Quaid, a character actor but not a "star," couldn't carry an entire movie as Chevy had done. There were also many problems with Quaid's wife on the set, but that story's been told and retold.

But for sure, *Animal House* begat the *Vacation* movies

and every other movie I've done, just as the *National Lampoon* begat *Animal House* and *Weight Watchers Magazine* begat *The National Lampoon* and before that, *Signature* begat *Weight Watchers Magazine*. One can only guess whether the *Lampoon* would have continued in film if we hadn't come up a winner our first time out.

In the decade or so after *Animal House*, the five *Vacation* movies were enormously popular. I also made some that weren't.

Films I developed, like *Movie Madness*, were either not that good or, some say, suffered by comparison to the most popular *Lampoon* films in the mid-80s. The magazine was hurt seriously by boycotts by religious groups and the move to TV and film of many of its contributors.

I sold control of the company in 1989. It has not prospered. Those who bought the company were not well suited to manage either an entertainment enterprise or a publishing company, and *Lampoon* was both.

Still, *Animal House*'s legacy lives on in new forms. A company called 4th Row Films is, as of this writing, preparing a documentary on the *Lampoon* in its golden years, of which *Animal House* will inevitably play a part. There's also a team (that I belong to) that's preparing a Broadway musical version of the movie. That group includes the Tony winners Jeffrey Richards (*August: Osage County*, *Hair*, etc.), director Casey Nicholaw (*Book of Mormon*), and the theater magnate Jimmy Nederlander Jr., as well as Universal Studios.

When I first started toying with the idea of turning *Animal House* into a Broadway musical, I called Jack Black's manager and asked him if Jack would consider playing Bluto, Jack being a fine singer as well as a comedy actor. The response was one of excitement. "I'll talk to Jack about it today," I was told. "I'll call you tomorrow." The next day the manager called back. "Jack says it's a great idea, but he'd never try to follow Belushi in that role." You can easily understand his reservations.

Some say that the best years of the *Lampoon* have long been over but to quote a noted twentieth-century philosopher: "OVER? Nothing is over until we decide it is! Was it over when the Germans bombed Pearl Harbor? Hell no!" (Bluto Blutarsky, 1978.)

18

Karen Allen, thirty-four years later, is as pretty, bright, and charming as ever. She talked about the aftermath of *Animal House*: "It was like a big impact for all concerned. But in some cases it took a while," she said. "Little by little, they did pay attention to me because of *Animal House* but like most people, I had to do my due diligence. I did *Cruising* and *The Wanderers*. My big breakthrough was *Raiders of the Lost Ark* with Spielberg, but you know, aside from being recognized as Katy in *Animal House* and, of course, *Raiders*, I get so much recognition from a movie I did with Jeff Bridges called *Starman*. People seemed to really love that picture and working with Jeff was so great.

"In all, I guess I've done about thirty films," she continued. "Only a few years ago, I was in *The Perfect Storm*, which was a truly wonderful movie."

She smiles thinking about Bill Murray and Michael O'Donoghue, who she went on to work with in *Scrooged*. "I remember one morning at six-thirty A.M., I'm sitting in the makeup trailer getting my hair done when Bill Murray wanders in and asks, "What are we shooting today?" I tell him and he takes the script from my hand and throws it on the floor. "I hate this scene!" he yelled and I kind of drew back. I had no idea what his next reaction would be. He just screamed, "I won't do it!" Then he walked over to the other side of the trailer and sat down and he kept saying, "I won't do it! I won't do it!" I asked the hairdresser to go get the director, Richard Donner. He arrived almost immediately and there in the trailer, in front of me and the makeup person and assistants, they started arguing about the scene. Finally, Richard called for a production assistant and told him to get Michael O'Donoghue. Michael was staying in a hotel near the set, so he arrived fifteen minutes later in his pajamas and slippers and an old bathrobe. And Michael and Bill sat there, argued, and rewrote the scene, finally, to Bill's satisfaction."

She also had a theatrical turn on Broadway. "I did a play called *Monday After the Miracle*. I played Helen Keller, who was both deaf and blind, and the story has been told many times in books, theater, and in film, where Patty Duke played the role and Anne Bancroft played the woman, Anne Sullivan, who taught her how to communicate with the rest of the world. That part was an incredible challenge and a beautiful play. After the play, I went to Paris and shot a film called *Until September*."

Karen got married in 1988 and her son Nicholas was born in 1990.

"I took some years off from acting after Nicholas was

born and moved to Massachusetts. I wanted to be with my son. Then I started Karen Allen Fine Arts, a knitting store and studio. I've always loved clothing design and now I have a store in town and a studio next to my home. Now, my son is in school in New York and I'm back acting, and have been for a few years."

In 2010, she attended the Toronto Film Festival, where a movie she had starred in, *White Irish Drinkers,* was well received. It brought her back together with Peter Riegert, who co-starred in the film. Recently, Peter described life after *Animal House* like this: "Well, I was like thirty at the time but nobody is prepared for the kind of success we all had after the movie became such an icon. Some years after that, I worked with Burt Lancaster on *Local Hero* and asked him about the business. He was probably one of the first actors to start his own production company. It was Hecht-Lancaster and they produced movies like *Marty* and *Sweet Smell of Success.* "You know, Peter," he said to me, "an actor needs an audience and you have to get lucky and be in something that's nationally known so your face and your name are a match. So you're an actor who people look at on screen or in the newspaper and say, 'Oh, I know who he is,' but they don't. It's very competitive and it's a big fucking culture that we live in." I'll always remember that phrase. He was saying that because here I'd come off this movie that everybody saw or has seen since it opened and my face was recognizable.

The notoriety of *Animal House* did throw me off. I was used to walking out of the theater and maybe having people who were leaving stop and tell me what they thought of the performance. Doing *Animal House* was like going from zero to mach three in half a minute. I always used to joke after the movie that I could have gotten room and board and the farmer's daughter in any town in the country. I happened to be living with somebody at the time but I could have fucked my way from New York to Los Angeles and back again anytime I wanted to. It was like an aphrodisiac, not just for me but for the people who saw it.

So it was overwhelming for me in the beginning because it was hard to understand, and I know this is going to sound absurd, but for somebody who's in the business of being watched, it was odd to be watched so often and everywhere I went. For a month I couldn't perform with my improv group, and when they asked me what the problem was I said that I felt like people were watching me, and they said, 'Well, they *are*, you idiot, you're on stage.' 'No, the wall is broken down for me. I can't get into the character. I've lost the acting concept.' It took me that month to put it into perspective."

In addition to *Local Hero*, Peter went on to perform in the films *Crossing Delancey*, *Traffic*, *The Mask*, and *Oscar*, as well as on TV.

"Yeah," he recalled. "I've done thirty, maybe forty films. Lots of theater, lots of television. The fact that I still pay the rent doing this is an achievement in itself. It's funny but what is *Animal House* except a story about a group of people who have no idea that what they're doing is self-destructive and they certainly don't take rejection seriously. All they see is a way forward to win in the end. One of Tim's speeches in the film says it all: 'What this calls for is a really stupid and futile gesture on somebody's part and we're just the guys to do it.'

"And that's exactly what it is to be an actor. It's having that audacity, maybe even stupidity, in a way, to think that you're going to go out and create a life for yourself in a world as muddy as show business. You know, it takes some kind of wacky person to do it."

Thom Mount and Sean Daniel, the studio executives who championed *Animal House*, have gone on to remarkably co-incidental careers. Thom replaced Ned Tanen as President of Productions at Universal, left in 1984, and was replaced by Sean.

Mount's first picture was *Bull Durham*, after which he produced *Natural Born Killers*. He's currently the president of Reliant Pictures.

Allegedly, Thom Mount was the inspiration for the Hollywood novel *The Player*, written by Michael Tolkin and later turned into a film directed by Robert Altman, starring Tim Robbins. Tolkin, before that, had been one of the staff writers on the *Lampoon* TV show *Delta House*. Of course, Tolkin's use of Mount to inspire the character did not include the murder depicted in the film.

As for Sean, after he left Universal, he formed his own production company. His first film was the notable *Dazed and Confused*. Then came *Tombstone*, *The Jackal*, and the hugely successful *Mummy* series. Like Mount, he is still actively producing.

•   •   •

After *Animal House*, Tim Matheson was a star. He looked at his options. "I knew I could have my own television series," he later told a reporter, "and pull in thirty or forty thousand dollars a week but I decided the way to go was more film." The first one he did almost immediately after *Animal House* was a long stretch from the "tasteless" college film: Disney's *The Apple Dumpling Gang Rides Again*.

Soon after that movie opened he was awakened at six one morning by his agent, who was calling to say that Steven Spielberg wanted him to be the lead in a film he was making, *1941*.

"I couldn't believe it," Matheson told the interviewer. "I was going from Disney to Spielberg. Apparently, Steven was screening *Animal House* at his home regularly and going nuts over it."

Tim also knew that Spielberg had frequently worn *Animal House* T-shirts after the movie came out. He was, quite obviously, a fan of the movie.

A headline in *Interview* magazine at the time read: "Tim Matheson is Mr. Wonderful, Even His Mother Says So." But *1941* wasn't wonderful. It became one of Spielberg's few flops.

Tim went on to star in *Up the Creek, A Very Brady Sequel, She's All That*, and most recently he went back to college, or at least to visit one, so to speak, in the film *Van Wilder*, in which he played Ryan Reynolds's character's dad. The movie was moderately successful, and did very well on DVD. But it was nonetheless refreshing to see Tim in a film about a college three decades later.

In 1978, Ned Tanen explained how some of the highest-grossing films at the box office often take on a life of their own. Describing the success of *Animal House*, he said, "It was a surprise. All we did was make a little picture about college fraternity life in the 1960s."

Tanen wasn't always the staunchest ally of *Animal House* during the making of the film, but it is worth noting that in the 1970s, under his supervision, Universal made such blockbuster films as *American Graffiti, Jaws, Smokey and the Bandit,* and *Missing.* His films, in 1980, set an industry box office receipts record of $290 million with releases including *Coal Miner's Daughter, The Blues Brothers,* and *Smokey and the Bandit 2.* He resigned from Universal in December 1982 and moved to Paramount Pictures in 1984. While head of production there he green-lighted and supervised *Crocodile Dundee, Top Gun, Fatal Attraction,* and *Beverly Hills Cop 2.* Again, under his supervision the studio posted the top revenues among all studios in both 1986 and 1987. In 1988 receipts topped $600 million.

Other films produced by Paramount while Ned was there included *Ferris Bueller's Day Off, Children of a Lesser God, The Accused,* and *Ghost.* He resigned in 1988. He was quite ill for a long time after that, passing away at the age of seventy-seven on January 5, 2009.

Ned Tanen was the toughest studio boss I ever worked with, but he lived movies, he loved movies, and his record speaks for itself. He was difficult to work with on *Animal House*, but because he was so demanding it wound up a better movie.

Deborah Nadoolman did all the costumes for the movie and her work added immeasurably to its success. Deborah had already been credited as a costume designer and was a member of that guild when she was asked to do *Animal House*, but the studio, with its small budget, insisted that she couldn't have the title or the pay of a costume designer. Instead, she took a credit that read "Costumes by Deborah Nadoolman."

She worked for us on a picture shot fifteen years after the time period in which it was set, with a budget of $50,000. Her next picture was Steven Spielberg's *1941*, her costume budget for that was $350,000, and she did it with the title "costume designer." On *Animal House*, Nadoolman worked exhaustive days and came up with funny ideas for clothing and innovative ways to save money and keep the period-look honest.

For instance, there's the opening scene at Omega House with the girls in their prom dresses. Buying dresses for all the girls in that scene would have been much too expensive. So Deborah designed the dresses and went to a Mexican wedding shop in downtown Los Angeles and had them made on the cheap. When she needed hundreds of pairs of sandals for the toga scene, she and Judy Belushi sat on a porch of the house that Judy and John had rented in Eugene and spray-painted every sandal gold. When she made the togas they were designed with comedic effect in mind. Every girl wore a bra under the toga and each was a different color so when the togas slipped a little we'd see different colors of bras. Otter's toga included a cape; this was actually a red checkered tablecloth from a restaurant. Bluto's was majestic because Deborah saw in him a power that said to her "Roman emperor." The wreath was included in the costume he was wearing when he was photographed for the cover of *Newsweek*. When Belushi strode down those stairs to destroy Steven Bishop's guitar, you knew that he felt the same power that the costumer had in mind.

She researched sixties yearbooks, the first one being Chris Miller's. In them she found exactly what the undergrads were wearing at that time. But she didn't have the budget for their clothes. So she hunted around and finally, at Disneyland, found the checkered jacket that Otter wears when he gives the speech at their trial in front of the dean and that great red sweater he wears in other scenes. If clothes make the man, Deborah's work helped make Otter's character.

You probably don't notice it when you watch the movie but it rained all the time in Eugene. For a good part of each day Deborah stood by the camera holding an open umbrella in one hand.

Deborah went on to such films as *Coming to America*, *Raiders of the Lost Ark*, and *An American Werewolf in London*. She is the president of the Costume Designer's Guild and is married to John Landis.

John Vernon, the veteran character actor, read a few passages of the script and we knew he was the perfect choice for our villain, Dean Wormer. He had been a dear friend since *Animal*

House. He liked to play the grumpy old man but he was a warm family man who had many close friends. One time, one of those friends said to him, "You know, John, sometimes I think I'm a curmudgeon too, just like you." John turned and gave him the Dean Wormer look of disdain. "You're not old enough," he snorted, "or smart enough to be a curmudgeon."

John had five kids, two of them now beautiful young women: Kate Vernon, a successful actress, and Nan Vernon, a singer and model. When Nan was in her late teens, John walked into her bedroom and discovered her in bed with her boyfriend. The boyfriend told the story at Vernon's memorial after his death in 2005. "Can you imagine the feeling," he asked us, "being in bed with Dean Wormer's daughter and he walks in?"

John appeared in dozens of films after *Animal House*, mostly playing the villain. With a voice that was one of the most recognizable in the entertainment world, he did many voice-overs, narrations, and commercials as well.

During the production of the *Animal House* television spin off *Delta House*, John came to my office, clearly unhappy, and asked if we could talk. "It's the script," John said. "It's got some problems."

I said, "Of course, let's talk about it."

He said, "Well, actually it's got one particular problem. It stinks!"

We dumped the script.

A few years before he died, we worked together on a children's movie I wrote and produced, *Baby Huey's Great Easter Adventure.* He played a grammar school principal much in the Dean Wormer vein.

• • •

Before *Animal House*, Verna Bloom had established herself as a dramatic actress in a number of films. The scene in which she's very drunk at home with the dean after being with Otter at the Delta party was partly improvised by Verna. Landis told her to go with it and she did. After *Animal House* she appeared in such movies as *After Hours* and *The Last Temptation of Christ*.

Look up the word "smarmy" in the dictionary and you won't find a reference to Greg Marmalard, but you should. James Daughton's portrayal of Omega president Greg Marmalard was so perfect, so on target, that young men everywhere stopped wearing ties and jackets, mussed their hair a little, and relaxed, rather than be anything like the character Daughton created. He is not a smarmy guy. He just played one in the movies, and has played that role many times since *Animal House*, obviously because he does it so well. Those movies included *Sorority Boys*, *Spies Like Us*, and *Mad About You*.

Cesare Danova, a serious dramatic actor, like Vernon and Bloom, played the role of Mayor DePasto with broad comedic sensibilities. Before and after the film he did a great deal of television, invariably playing the guy with a scowl and a gun. He passed away in 1992.

After *Animal House*, for John Landis, came *Trading Places*, *The Blues Brothers*, *An American Werewolf in London*, *Coming to America*, *¡Three Amigos! Spies Like Us* (with *Lampoon* graduate Chevy Chase), and *Twilight Zone: The Movie*, and more.

Both Landis and Ivan Reitman have created pictures on anyone's list of favorite comedies; Ivan with *Stripes* and John with Eddie Murphy, Dan Ackroyd, Don Ameche, and Ralph Bellamy in *Trading Places*.

As notable was John's direction of Michael Jackson's *Thriller*, considered by most to be the best music video ever made.

John has done outstanding work directing musical sequences. The "Shout!" scene certainly speaks of that, but think of *The Blues Brothers*—one great musical number after another.

In early 2011, Landis was given a Lifetime Achievement Award at the tenth Monte Carlo Film Festival in Monaco. At the same festival they screened his latest, *Burke and Hare*. It's about time for this director to come back to studios to make pictures. He is an overwhelming presence (I readily admit that I have complained about that at times), but this is his personality, and that power and presence and personality is what makes him John Landis.

"What's interesting about *Animal House*," Mark Metcalf said years later, "is that whenever you do a picture, especially if you're on location away from home and just there for a while, you build relationships with people you work with. You kind of bond with them, whenever you do a picture or a play. It's one of the main reasons to do it. You sort of create this new family. And after filming and the Omega-Delta stuff was all cleaned up and everybody realized that it was strictly a Landis ploy that worked, we bonded with everyone again and again and again. It's been a long time and people are still talking about it, and we're still talking to each other about it. It's really a thrill to see the movie now and realize it works like a dream.

I did a movie called *One Crazy Summer* with Demi Moore and John Cusack and a critic in the *Los Angeles Times* gave it a really bad review. '*Animal House* started this trend toward raunchy comedy and hopefully,' he wrote, '*One Crazy Summer* will end it.' Obviously, it didn't end it but I felt really proud to have been there at the beginning and, according to the critic, the end.

"I'm still making movies," Metcalf continued, "mostly as a villain, and there's a whole generation of people who still think of me as Niedermeyer but also know me from the Twisted Sister videos. They always want me to scream at them, 'What do you want to do with your life?' That was the punch line in the videos, but they're not really happy unless I spit on them, like I did on Flounder in the ROTC scene, or scream in their face and say, 'Is that a pledge pin on your uniform?'

"I've gotten death threats in the mail from people who didn't like Niedermeyer. When I get them I figure I've done my job really well.

"I had another friend who went to the U.S. Naval Academy in Annapolis and they said before the movie came out they used to call all their drill instructors 'asshole'—behind their backs, of course. But after the movie came out they started calling them 'Niedermeyer.'"

In recent years, Mark has done film, television, and theater but immediately after *Animal House*, instead of trying to push his acting career, he got deeply involved in producing a feature film with two friends of his, Griffin Dunne and Amy Robertson. The movie was *Chilly Scenes of Winter,* a low-budget film which, he notes, "was probably seen by one one-hundredth of the people who saw *Animal House.*" Peter Riegert, who had been a friend of Mark's in New York, was in it, as was John Heard and Mary Beth Hurt.

"I was so busy doing the film that I really wasn't thinking about what my career might have been if I'd worked on trying to get acting roles after *Animal House* came out. As a matter of fact, when it became a hit, I started to become more in demand as an actor but I turned everything down because I was producing the movie. That," he concedes, "was not really a bright move. I wasn't thinking about my career. I just was thinking about what interested me most at the time."

One of the most clever scenes in the movie takes place when the Deltas go on their road trip. Otter has read in the town paper that one of the undergraduates at the nearby girl's school, Dickenson, had died in a kiln explosion. He decides he and his friends need dates, so they stop off at Dickenson. He enters the dorm and asks for the girl, obviously acting as though he didn't know she died. Her roommate, played by Lisa Baur, comes down to solemnly tell Otter, "That dear Fawn Liebowitz is dead." Obviously attracted to each other they sit on a bench and she takes his hand to try to ease the pain.

"My God," he says in a voice that oozed with pain, "we were engaged to be engaged. She was making a pot for me."

Now came the line that particularly struck me. She nods and says softly, "I know. She told me."

Obviously, her deceased roommate never told the girl about her because she'd never seen or heard of Otter but Lisa Baur, was so cool for responding in that manner that it brought enormous laughter from audiences.

Lisa apparently stopped performing after that.

Stephen Bishop still tours and writes songs, his most famous being "On and On."

Kevin Bacon, appearing as Chip, the Omega house pledge, became and remains a major star, but even after *Animal House* it wasn't easy at first.

"Well, I thought, okay, I've made a movie. Now I'm in but I wasn't in," he recalled. "So I started all over again. I went back to my old job as a waiter instead of going back to acting school. I started auditioning and I got an agent. That's certainly something the movie prompted me to do. Having been in what had almost immediately become an iconic movie did make people take a good look at me. Once I went to the auditions and they saw *Animal House* on my résumé they always were interested. I'll always carry those memories with me."

Footloose was the movie, more than any after *Animal House*, that set him on his way.

"My advice is," he said, "if you can do anything else, do it. It's a heartbreaking business. If the wannabe says, 'Fuck you, I'm gonna do it anyway!' then that's the attitude they'll have to have. If they say, 'Well, I'm gonna try it and see if it'll work,' then they're in the wrong career. You should only do it if it's the only thing you want to do and you're ready to deal with the heartbreaks."

His film credits run on forever but they include *Diner, Mystic River, Sleeping Dogs, Flatliners, Apollo 13,* and dozens more. He's married to the film and TV star Kyra Sedgwick, who has appeared for several years now on the popular TV show *The Closer.* They live in New York City and have two kids. When not performing in film, he plays in a rock band, The Bacon Brothers.

John Belushi's wife, Judy, appeared in only two scenes in the film but off-screen she was everywhere. She worked with Deborah Nadoolman on costumes. She helped scout locations and found the bathroom where the pot scene was shot in. The house she lived in with John in Eugene was the place that the other actors came to to relax—the few times they did relax.

Judy was always there and always ready. Apparently the day she and John met Bruce McGill at JFK airport in New York and boarded a plane to Oregon, they buckled up, sat back, had a drink, and relaxed. Some twenty minutes out of New York, the pilot announced that the plane had engine trouble and they had to return to JFK. When they got there and the passengers left the plane, they were told that the only other flight to Oregon that day was fully booked and they couldn't leave until the next day. Judy turned to Bruce and John and said, "Stay here!" She then sprinted toward the manager's office, threw open the door, and said, "I'm here with two actors who are starring in a multimillion-dollar Universal picture. Shooting starts first thing tomorrow morning. If we can't leave today the studio will lose a million dollars. They must get on that plane!"

Twenty minutes later, all three were on a plane en route to Oregon. (In fact, the filming wasn't starting for four days.)

Judy can be tough and firm when it's called for, but she points out, "I was younger then and when you're young you fear nothing and will do anything." She seems to have stayed pretty strong. Since John's death, she invested wisely in the House of Blues nightclubs, has written several books about John, and produced a number of biographical documentaries. Currently, she's planning another film with one of the major studios.

Some years after John's death, she remarried, and at the time of this writing is getting divorced. She has a son by her second marriage. She's also currently coproducing and acting in a musical stage show written by Rhonda Coullet, who was in the second company of *Lemmings* and who has remained close to Judy through all these years.

Judy Belushi stood by her guy through the great times and the troubled times.

If Landis's description of the movie as being sweet can be found anywhere, it's in the actor Stephen Furst and the character, Flounder, he created. He readily tells you now after a long career as a successful actor and director, that his life turned 180 degrees from being a starving actor to being: "Well, I don't want to say I'm famous but I'm well-known." He's apparently still famous enough to do national television commercials and is a huge draw at autograph shows where they talk about his TV roles but always ask him to add "Flounder" to his autograph.

After *Animal House*, Stephen was offered a lot of Disney movies. (They like "sweet.") He did a number of studio films including *Up the Creek* with Tim Matheson and then clicked big once again, this time on television, with *St. Elsewhere*. "Not only was it a hit show," he says, "it was a prestigious show. We all were considered 'actors.' You don't get that with Disney movies. I lucked out and, generally, I've been lucky. I think I'm a mediocre actor and Flounder was just the right part for me."

When we followed *Animal House* with the television show *Delta House*, Stephen was one of the first actors brought in to reprise his original role. *Delta House* was of course one of the *Lampoon* projects that really didn't work. Stephen offered his slant on the show.

"It was interesting to me. Every network was doing a fraternity show and I had an offer from each of them. I still wasn't being offered the big money. CBS had *Co-ed Fever*, NBC had *Brothers and Sisters*, and ABC had *Delta House*, and they were basically all offering the same money. Maybe I was getting a little bit more than the other actors because I did have an offer from all the networks. I decided to stick with the people that did *Animal House*, there's a loyalty factor, but there's also a quality factor, and we lasted the longest. Only one episode of *Co-ed Fever* was aired and their lead-in was the Super Bowl. How bad could that show have been when your lead-in is the Super Bowl? *Brothers and Sisters* lasted about twelve episodes and *Delta House* lasted thirteen. We were constantly being hamstrung by the network: It was television and we just couldn't be *Animal House*. So, I was very disappointed but not disappointed enough to make me forget how wonderful it was to be part of *Animal House*."

In addition to *St. Elsewhere*, Stephen was one of the stars of *Babylon 5*, which was so successful, its reruns still appear on cable stations. For years afterward, Stephen and other members of that cast have gone to science fiction conventions and autographed thousands of photos. He says, however, although photographs were of him as his *Babylon 5* character, people would constantly talk about Flounder.

Bruce McGill, who started acting in theater, says that acting in films is harder. "The difference," he explains, "is that for a film you must make all the major decisions about the character before they take the first shot. For the stage, you can often change the character as the plot progresses. Film must always be consistent. A stage actor has to project his feelings, which can be much harder on film. The camera does the projecting. This is why some people can't make it in films, even though they do well on the stage. They insist on projecting to the camera and it comes off as overacting."

McGill is another actor who emphasized that Deborah Nadoolman's selection of clothes certainly helped make his role stronger.

Over the years, he's seen the movie four times. "The first time I saw it, I was aware of scenes that had been cut, thinking, oh, that's gone. The second time I was less clued in to the details and I had certain reservations as I watched it. The third time, I was sitting in an audience of complete strangers who were really enjoying it. It was the most fun I had ever had in a movie theater. And the fourth time I saw it, I really loved it."

Among his many film credits are *Courage Under Fire, A Line in the Sand, Collateral,* and *Silkwood.*

Soon after *Animal House* and the aborted *Delta House,* Jamie Widdoes, Delta president Hoover, turned TV director and producer, so he's still trying to keep people in tow. As such, he's been involved with *Empty Nest, Boston Common, The King of Queens,* and *Two and a Half Men,* for which he directed nearly 60 episodes. It's interesting to note that shortly after *Animal House,* Widdoes did an interview for his hometown newspaper, *The Pittsburgh Post Gazette,* in which he was quoted as saying, "I don't know much about filmmaking but I'm studying it, I'm trying to learn the craft." Obviously he's an apt pupil.

It was difficult to guess which of the young actors in *Animal House* would go on to become stars. Tim Matheson seemed to be a cinch, as did Tom Hulce and Peter Riegert. We all knew that Karen Allen would make it, and certainly all the others would go on to be, if not stars, successful featured players, and for the most part they did. Another actress we felt was certainly going to be a star was Sarah Holcomb, who played Clorette, the thirteen-year-old daughter of Mayor DePasto. She was beautiful, smart, and talented. She went on to be the leading lady in *Caddyshack,* then played opposite Robby Benson in *Walk Proud,* and finally in, *Happy Birthday, Gemini.*

My own path crossed with hers during the making of *National Lampoon's Vacation*. We were filming the camping scene and Brian Doyle-Murray was playing a cameo as the camp owner. He arrived with Sarah. I'd already heard that she had gotten deeply into drug use.

When I saw her those few days on location in Colorado, she looked tired. She was still in her early twenties but didn't have the flair and vivaciousness that we'd seen in her first movies. The drug use was taking its toll. I didn't hear about her again until many, many years later. We talked about her at get-togethers and people always asked about her. There is no question that she had a problem with addiction, and she dropped out of film because of it. Chris Miller probably summed it up best: "She was much younger than we were on *Animal House* and I suppose she was too young to handle that scene." In 2004, a film called *Stateside* was about a young actress who had succeeded in her first movies and was on her way to becoming a star when she suddenly got lost in the drug scene, and simply disappeared. The picture was clearly about Sarah Holcomb. David Holcomb played the leading lady's brother. In addition, there was a thank you at the end of the film to "S.H."

Years later, a young conductor who worked on the New York Central told of being on a train when it pulled into the Stamford train yards. He and the engineer were the only ones on board. Suddenly he saw a young woman, obviously in her mid-twenties, sleeping in the corner of one of the cars. She was blond and pretty, and she startled when he woke her. She had fallen asleep and missed her station and said that somebody was there waiting for her. The conductor told her that his car was just outside the train yards and he would drive her back to the station.

As they drove they talked, and there was something about her that stoked his memory. Finally, he asked, "What do you do for a living?" She told him she was an actress and he knew then that it was Sarah Holcomb. He later checked with a friend who thought they had known her, and after an Internet search discovered that she is now living a quiet, obscure life under a different name, far from Hollywood. He also had heard that Sarah does not wish to be found.

Tom Hulce was Pinto, the everyman in the movie. For the most part, if you were in a fraternity, or just hung out with a bunch of guys, you were or knew Pinto. He was later a standout in *Dominic and Eugene* and received an Academy Award nomination for his role as *Amadeus*. He has done a number of other films since then but more recently has concentrated mainly on teaching and theater production. As of this writing, he's preparing a show for Broadway.

After *Animal House*, Mary Louise Weller appeared in a number of films, including *Forced Vengeance*, playing Chuck Norris's girlfriend, which, after playing opposite Otter, is like dancing with a chair. Mostly, it's been TV work and a lot of it, including *Quincy*, *Kojak*, and *Starsky and Hutch*. She now lives on a ranch in Malibu and raises horses.

Martha Smith says people still call her Babs. "I have a recurring role in a show called *Greek*, a sorority/fraternity show. My character is the president of the sorority, and the sorority color is pink, so when I first appeared on the show, they wanted to dress me in pink and it was like I was playing a grown-up Babs. They were so excited to have me in the cast. The script has me repeating some lines from *Animal House*, like, probably my most famous line, 'That boy is a P-I-G, pig!"

Since *Animal House*, Martha's acting career has been mostly on television. Her most notable role was perhaps as Francine, Kate Jackson's costar in the series *The Scarecrow and Mrs. King*, in which she appeared in eighty-nine episodes.

She continues to act on television, dividing her time between that and selling Beverly Hills real estate, which ain't bad real estate to share your career with.

Before *Animal House,* a very young Martha Smith had appeared in *Playboy*. In 2007 that magazine put out a limited edition of their best Playmate photos, in which "Babs" was featured. She points out that although she was one of 48 in that edition, *Playboy* has actually published 15 million photographs over the years. So, actually, she was 1 out of 48 out of 15 million.

Otis Day and the Knights, and in particular their rendition of "Shout!" became so popular after the movie that DeWayne Jessie changed his stage name to Otis Day, formed a new band, and since 1979 has toured colleges and clubs all over the world. He's also often seen on stage in Las Vegas clubs.

There is no more versatile member of the film industry than Harold Ramis. He has succeeded as an actor, writer, director, and producer. His list of credits, if recorded, would create a paper trail from his hometown, Chicago, to Los Angeles. His acting credits include *Stripes*, the *Ghostbuster* films, Judd Apatow's *Knocked Up*, and a dozen or so others. "Easy to like" is what Ramis is, and that calm personality, combined with the ability to make the right decisions, an obvious superior sense of humor, and an aura that says "I may be quiet but I'm in charge," has led to his success. In addition to his acting, he cowrote and appeared in *Stripes* and the *Ghostbuster* films, and directed *National Lampoon's Vacation*, *Caddyshack*, *Groundhog Day*, *Analyze This*, and *Analyze That*. He cowrote and directed Chris Miller's film *Multiplicity*, one of the most clever and underrated comedies in recent decades.

Harold and his family now live in Chicago because he has never lost his love for the city.

Ramis is the perfect collaborator. In addition to coming up with great ideas and lines, he knows how to listen. He and Doug and Chris listened to each other and exchanged ideas. And he continues to do that. Most of the writing he has done in film has been collaborative and almost all of it has been successful. His box office record speaks to his talent as a director. *Groundhog Day* and *Vacation* are constantly rated among the best comedies ever.

Chris Miller went on to write the scripts for *Multiplicity*, story for *Club Paradise*, and many TV shows, as well as a number of bestselling books. His book *The Real Animal House*, describes the genesis of what became the Delta's story.

In a 1979 article in the *Louisiana Courier-Express*, Bob Groves detailed Miller's thinking about "gross-out" humor:

Chris Miller, a *NatLamp* writer and co-author of the screenplay for the movie *Animal House,* variously describes the gross-out point as the button, "the paranoid episode," or the point of "this time they've gone too far."

"I'm going to advance a theory," Miller announced, "of what happens to people who really get upset, about what button has been pushed. . . . I call it the Paranoid Episode. It happens unexpectedly.

"Everybody, except a few swamis, lives their lives with illusions because being in touch with absolute truth would be destructive—death and life would be meaningless.

"So you find things that make life work and that's fine. But if something strips away illusions, you are totally vulnerable, like a one-year-old kid."

To illustrate his theory, Miller then produced a couple of samples of actual hate mail that comes into the *NatLamp* offices.

In the late 1980s, the *National Lampoon* magazine conducted a survey and in it Chris Miller's short stories were shown to be among the three most popular features in the magazine. He lives in LA and continues to write short stories for national magazines.

Doug Kenney was an unmistakable presence throughout the making of *Animal House,* as well as in the early years of the *Lampoon.* Certainly he was one of the three great humorists of the last thirty or forty years.

After Kenney left the *Lampoon* he produced *Caddyshack,* and the movie was wacky enough to prove that Doug had a large hand in it.

But according to *A Futile and Stupid Gesture: How Doug Kenney and National Lampoon Changed Comedy Forever*, a biography by Josh Karp, Doug hated *Caddyshack*. The day after the *Caddyshack* premiere in July 1980, Warner Bros. scheduled a press conference at Dangerfield's (Rodney's club) in New York. Chevy, Harold, Brian Doyle-Murray, Stephanie and Harry Kenney (Doug's parents), and others were there. The publicist opened by asking the audience, "Wasn't it great?" and then added jokingly, "And who thought it sucked?"

An agitated Doug burst into applause from the back of the room. "Yeah, it sucked!" he yelled. "Didn't everyone think it was terrible?" The publicist tried to take the focus off Doug and said, "He's joking!" The Kenneys got up from their seats, Doug's mother hugged him, his father put his arm around his son's shoulder, and they led him out of the room.

Karp writes that this incident led someone to suggest to Chevy that Doug needed to dry out and rest. This suggestion led in turn to a vacation in Hawaii.

Before *Caddyshack*, Doug had met Kathryn Walker at a party in New York. He was so taken with her that he got her attention by calmly eating a crystal glass. Kathryn was a successful actress and quite attractive and smart. He, of course, was attractive and smart too, and successful and funny, if erratic. They fell in love and moved to Los Angeles where they rented a home in pricey Coldwater Canyon. Doug, at Kathryn's insistence, made an effort to cure his drug addiction, but during *Caddyshack* he was a wild man. In an *Esquire* article about Doug published in 1981, friends are quoted about his cocaine habit. "What he dropped on the floor," said one, "would keep most people high for a lifetime." Another described his lust for the drug this way: "He went after it like an animal in heat—stuffing it into his nose with his thumb, great gobs of it."

On the set of *Caddyshack* the word was that all the principals involved were high during most of the shoot except Ted Knight. Rodney Dangerfield had shown up two days before filming started with a large suitcase filled with drugs. Chevy came the next day with an even bigger one.

Robin Williams has said, "Cocaine is God's way of telling you you're making too much money." God spoke loudly on that shoot.

After *Caddyshack* Kathryn begged him to get help. He went to see a psychiatrist but returned only a few times. The reaction to *Caddyshack* gnawed at him. It simply wasn't *Animal House*. And he was, perhaps, too used to success. He went directly from college to being one of the people who created the most popular humor magazine of all time. He'd conceived and orchestrated the *High School Yearbook*, which critics still call a masterpiece. And he'd cowritten the movie comedy.

I saw Doug Kenney frequently after *Animal House* while I was at Universal. I went to parties at his home where cocaine flowed easily, and where my wife and I were among the few not using. He visited my home, where the service tended more to beer and booze. He would also drop by my studio office. One day he walked in and picked up a script that I had been reading. He glanced at the first few pages, as he had done at

Harold's apartment, and proceeded to tell me a complete story using the characters and plot lines introduced in the script he'd just looked at. I never moved with either story but the five-minute ad-lib was once again the better one.

After *Caddyshack* was released, he again stopped by my office in LA. He was feeling lousy about the film, blaming himself as though no one else had been involved. "Hey," I told him, "Billy Wilder made an occasional bad movie, too."

He looked at me and nodded, then said, "Yeah, but we invented nostalgia."

Despite his misgivings about the film, it has become a successful cult movie with a rabid fanbase.

In late August 1980, Doug was vacationing on the Hawaiian island of Kauai. Kathryn, Chevy, and other friends who had gone there with him had returned to the mainland. He stood alone on a cliff overlooking the Pacific. He then either walked out on a precipice, which crumbled under his feet, or he jumped. It is unclear which. His body was flown to Connecticut for a funeral. Kathryn and Chevy, who were the last people close to him to see and talk to him, insist that he did not commit suicide and that it was an accident.

At the *Lampoon*, one wag said what Doug would have said under similar circumstances: "He was looking for a place to jump off, when he slipped."

In his hotel room, he had written a note, supposedly to himself. "These are the happiest days I've ever ignored."

When the funeral services ended and Doug was buried, his best friend, Peter Ivers, stood alone at his gravesite and played a song on his harmonica. It was the classic "Beautiful Dreamer."

Like John Belushi, Doug was more than someone I worked with. He was like a son. We worked together for more than a decade, we disagreed a lot, but agreed more often. He was, truthfully, a good man, and like Belushi, whom we would lose soon after, he was good, but not strong.

I believe that he would have gone on to the same kind of success that John Hughes had. He had the same great story-telling talent, only wilder.

Linda Drucker wrote about Doug in the *Los Angeles Times* shortly after his death.

Kenney was writing a screenplay for another film par-ody when he accidentally fell to his death September 3 from a 30-foot cliff on the Hawaiian island of Kauai. He was 33.

Kenney remained true to the *Lampoon* image when he appeared at the graduation ceremony of the high school on which the *National Lampoon's High School Yearbook* was based and told the graduates that the real reason to go to college is "to study sex, alcohol, and dope."

Kenney was nonetheless deeply engaged with the world around him.

"Take an existentialist," Kenney said in 1978. "Add a hot Camaro, a skateboard, and a lot of dope, and you have a vital working existentialist who can get a job with the *National Lampoon*."

Did Doug nail it, both about the movie and his own life when, in the film, he had Donald Sutherland's Professor Jennings lecture in class about Milton's *Paradise Lost*? "Certainly," Jennings says, "we know he was trying to describe the struggle between good and evil. Right? Okay, the most intriguing character, as we all know from our reading, was Satan. Now, was Milton trying to tell us that being bad was more fun than being good?"

Neither Doug nor Jennings ever answered that question.

Longtime *Lampoon* contributor Stu Kreisman said after Doug's death, "I still can't come up with a rational explanation for Doug's death. The truth is that if he walked into my office tomorrow afternoon, it wouldn't surprise me a bit."

Ivan Reitman is not an actor or a screenwriter, but as a film director and producer he has been as successful and prolific as anyone in the history of the industry.

Immediately after *Animal House* he felt left out. "Matty and the *Lampoon* had gotten a great producing deal at Universal; John Landis was the hottest director in town; the writers had all sorts of offers and deals; and when it came to me, everybody said, 'Hey. If you ever get anything good, please show it to us.' That's what I got."

So Ivan, not garnering the same reaction as the others, called his friends in Canada. "I told them I had to start directing because there was no respect for producers in Hollywood. And so I did go back. I had only directed one low-budget film in my career, having produced quite a few others. I wanted to direct."

Meatballs, starring Bill Murray, started shooting two days after *Animal House* was released. After editing it, he screened it at a theater in LA and invited me to see it. As I walked out, Murray was in the lobby. He came up to me and asked what I thought. "I thought the picture was great," I said, "and you were sensational." And he was. Bill Murray's performance in *Meatballs* established him as a new comedy star. I put it up there with Belushi's Bluto, Dustin Hoffman's Tootsie, and Chevy Chase's Clark Griswold on my list of exceptional comedic performances. Murray had started with brief appearances as part of Second City, was a staff writer on the *Lampoon Radio Hour*, did some ensemble acting in the *Lampoon* stage show, replaced Chevy Chase on *Saturday Night Live*, and was now a star.

The film did well and it launched both Ivan's career and Bill Murray's. Ivan did his next film, *Stripes*, with Murray and Harold Ramis, and it was even more successful than *Meatballs*. He was on his way and has never stopped since.

He has produced and/or directed the *Ghostbuster* films, *Old School, Beethoven, Six Days Seven Nights*, and *Private Parts*, the latter starring Howard Stern, a film taken from his biography, which was, again coincidentally, co-written by another *Lampoon* alum, Larry "Ratso" Sloman. Ratso had been the last editor of the *Lampoon* under my ownership.

He made *Twins, Kindergarten Cop*, and *Junior* with Arnold Schwarzenegger, who has called him "the best comedy director that I ever worked with."

Most recently, Ivan directed *No Strings Attached*, with

Natalie Portman and Ashton Kutcher. By the time you read this, there will be several new Reitman movies at hand.

Then there's the incredibly lucky boy who during the parade scene was reading *Playboy*, then watches as a Playmate comes flying into his bedroom and he utters the memorable line, "Thank you, God!" In later years he became a pastor at the local church in Cottage Grove, Oregon. A story that appeared in the local paper when he was ordained read: "Lucky boy. Still thanking God."

19

BELUSHI: THE LEGEND LIVES

"How come," a friend once asked John Belushi, "you're so comfortable in front of a camera or on stage?"

"I guess," Belushi answered, "being in front of a camera or on stage are the two places where I always know what I'm going to do next."

That sums it up nicely. When he was on stage, he knew exactly what he was going to do but when he was off stage, he was spontaneous, unplanned, and unpredictable. On or off stage he needed to be noticed.

The late actor Richard Widmark once said a star "is someone who, when they're on screen or on stage, is the person you're looking at. Some people call it charisma, some people call it being a star, but whatever you call it, you are the center of attention." John was always the center of attention—and always wanted to be.

A couple of years back, John's star was put onto the Hollywood Walk of Fame and many friends, family, and fellow actors attended the ceremony. Dan Ackroyd was there, as was John and Dan's agent, Bernie Brillstein. Judy had asked me to attend, so I did. John's brother, Jim, spoke about their grand-mother, who raised them from the time they were very young because their parents worked long days and nights. John and Jim were both in their twenties when their grandmother died. At her funeral, hundreds of friends, relatives, and people from the Albanian community in Chicago showed up. John sud-denly saw that Jim was in a corner by himself, crying. He angrily walked over to his younger brother. "Stop it!" he com-manded. "This is no time for that. You're a man. Act like a man!" Jim nodded and straightened up. A few minutes later, Jim looked around and saw that a large circle of mourners had gathered in the center of the room watching something with great interest. He walked over. It was John, sitting in the center of the circle with tears rolling down his cheeks and loud sobs coming from him. He was, indeed, the center of attention.

John couldn't help it. He was always a force, always in-tense, funny, dramatic—always "on." John was totally ab-sorbed in and dedicated to what he loved to do.

During the *Lemmings* days, I had a summer house in Westport, Connecticut, and on weekends I would invite the staff of the magazine and members of the cast and crew of the show to visit. I remember John barreling through the house, drinking, dancing to the loud music that was playing, and join-ing in the fun in the pool where we played volleyball, the boys against the girls. It was the early seventies and everybody had long hair, so after every weekend I had to have someone come in and strain the enormous amounts of hair out of the pool.

One Sunday afternoon, John thundered into the kitchen and roared, happily, "Where's the Southern Comfort?" Our housekeeper, Francine, smiled and looked at John and shouted, "Here I is!" She was as wide as John and he picked her up and hugged her and both of them fell to the floor laughing.

I remember those weekends so well. We played a lot of basketball. Chris Guest was a good player and Chevy could shoot a basket from almost any angle. I remember too that Michael O'Donoghue was a really good Ping-Pong player. But most of all, I remember John having fun. And I remember his appetite. At the end of the day I used to go out back and grill steaks for everyone. John was the only one who could eat three steaks. His appetite for food, and just about anything else, was boundless.

When O'Donoghue left the *Radio Show*, later to join *Saturday Night Live*, Belushi became the director. One of the programs he put on was called "The Death Penalty." It was a fierce attack on capital punishment. So fierce, we lost the one national advertiser we had, 7-Up, after complaints came in, particularly from the South and the middle of the country. That advertising was paying for the show. When I told John about it, he shrugged, smiled slyly, and said proudly, "Pretty good, huh? The show was so good I wiped out all our advertising."

Mark Metcalf recalls meeting John in Central Park in 1975. "It was right before *Saturday Night Live* started, and John Heard, who was my best friend at the time, and his girlfriend, and my girlfriend, the actress Pamela Reed, all went to see Shakespeare in the Park. The girls made fried chicken and some potato salad and we went to Central Park and we're laying there on the grass talking, drinking some wine, and having some chicken, and this big guy comes walking by. John Heard had spent some time in Chicago and he knew him and he said, 'John, come over here,' and introduced us to Belushi. None of us knew who John Belushi was at that time. We hadn't seen *Lemmings*.

"So, Belushi came over and sat down with us and we said, 'Have some chicken. What's going on?' And he went into this long story about how he'd been asked to audition for this live, late night television show, supposed to be all comedy, and he didn't want to do it because television was 'horrible, just terrible' and he stood up on this guy, Lorne Michaels's desk, and was telling him how he hated television. I guess Lorne Michaels was real calm through all of this and said, 'Well, listen, if you don't like it, the only way to change the system is to work inside it and that's what we're gonna do, so come on and do it too.' And Belushi spent half an hour telling us about this and trying to get our advice on whether he should do this thing or not and then finally he got up and wandered off and we realized that all the time he'd been talking, and we'd been listening and talking back and forth and asking questions and having this animated conversation, he'd been eating—and all our chicken and potato salad was gone! Our advice to him had been, 'Come on, they're going to pay you American money— go do it!'"

Landis recalls directing John in *Animal House* and other projects. "His face was so amazing that if you look at his part, the entrances and exits, he just comes in and out but he makes it so funny. He and I worked great together and I started directing him while the camera was rolling. I would talk him through stuff and he would instantly do it, then I'd just remove my voice. Like, you know where he walks down the food line in the cafeteria? That was not rehearsed. And the 'Peeping Tom' scene where he's on the ladder? I decided to break the fourth wall and have him look at the camera because with that arched eyebrow, John made the entire audience coconspirators."

The director thinks Belushi was a cross between Harpo Marx and the Cookie Monster. He felt Harpo had a sweetness about him, and yet he was completely destructive. The cafeteria scene in which he jams all of that food down his mouth is pure Harpo gone mad. The Cookie Monster, like Bluto, is gruff with a prodigious appetite. Of course, John was all of those things in real life—destructive, gruff, with a huge appetite for everything, yet very sweet.

Landis still marvels at John's ability to "speak" without uttering a word, using only facial movements and subtle gestures. "Eugene, Oregon, where we shot the film, was the home of the noted author Ken Kesey. Belushi was a big fan and Kesey invited him to his home." Landis accompanied him. "Kesey went on and on about the 'Killer Bees' sketch from *Saturday Night Live*—a sketch that Belushi hated, but Kesey wouldn't stop talking about it. Belushi sat alongside the writer as he spoke, and when Kesey turned to talk to me, Belushi would make those Oliver Hardy looks behind his back. You know, those looks of anguish and disgust.

"A moment I treasure," Landis recalls, "is when I finally screened the film for John and Judy at Universal: They watched it by themselves and I was waiting in the parking lot. He comes up and gives me this incredible bear hug, I mean, broke my back, and then held my face like a Jewish mother and said, 'Do you know what you've done for me, John?' And I said, 'What?' And he said, 'You've made me far too expensive to ever work with *you* again!'"

After *Animal House*, Belushi turned his attention to the Blues Brothers and with Dan Ackroyd performed live with a collection of jazz all-stars. Belushi and Ackroyd owned the rights to the Blues Brothers characters and decided they'd make a movie, which Ackroyd would write based on the adventures of the two Chicago-based characters, Jake and Elwood Blues. Landis agreed to direct it.

Before filming *The Blues Brothers*, John had gained so much weight that his belly hung well over his belt. Landis, who was to direct the movie, talked him into going to La Costa, the health resort where you pay obscenely high prices to dine on carrots and lemon water.

After a few days there, Landis was congratulating himself on Belushi's adherence to the resort's discipline. At dinner he'd wolf down the celery and wafer-thin entrees and remark on their tastiness. On the third night, Landis knocked on Belushi's door around midnight to tell him about an idea he'd come up with for the film. There was no answer. Concerned, he turned the door handle and, discovering that the room was unlocked, he entered. It was empty. He turned to leave. As he did, he heard a noise at the window. He saw that it was Belushi and snapped on the lights. Under John's burly arms were a foot-long salami, a loaf of Italian bread, and a bagful of condiments and other goodies. When he saw Landis, he smiled his charming, sheepish grin. "Just dropped down to the general store in town," he said. "A man needs nourishment." When they left La Costa, Landis, who wasn't overweight to start with, had lost four pounds. Belushi had gained one.

They went on to shoot *The Blues Brothers*. Landis describes it as a tough shoot, and for the first time Belushi's excesses came into play during the filming of a movie. John had been clean, sober, on time, and always prepared on the set of *Animal House*. Now things were beginning to change. "It was a good thing he wore those dark glasses," Landis told me. "Without them you could see what was going on at night and in between shots."

The Blues Brothers grossed just under $30 million in North America, but, surprisingly, did a terrific $60 million at foreign box offices. John had caught on internationally. The movie would later earn most of its money on cable and video, again all over the world. It did well enough that in 2000 Universal agreed to make *Blues Brothers 2000*. John Goodman played Jake and Ackroyd returned as Elwood. The movie was unsuccessful, however, grossing less than $15 million at the U.S. box office.

After *The Blues Brothers*, Belushi did two films in 1981: *Neighbors* and *Continental Divide*. In both films, he decided not to play "Bluto." *Neighbors* was a comedy and in it Dan Ackroyd played the comedy lead while John was the straight man, an obvious reversal of their Blues Brothers characters, and one that was ineffective. In *Continental Divide* with Blair Brown, John went "Spencer Tracy," underplaying the part of a traditional leading man in a romantic comedy. An *underplaying*

Belushi was not what audiences wanted. Although the performances by John and Brown were well received by the critics, the movie wasn't. Belushi said during the filming that he thought the director, Michael Apted, was bringing him down. "He keeps insisting that I be normal," said John, "and I want to be, but acting normal didn't have to mean that I didn't have a sense of humor. And the lack of that made the movie dull." John didn't do dull well.

In his book *Life*, Keith Richards talks about going on a spree with John and Mick Jagger in New York. Mick and Keith had been recording all night and had gone back to Mick's place. There was a knock on the door and Belushi joined them.

"When we were kids, I used to go to Mick's house and occasionally open the refrigerator and all that would ever be in it was half a tomato. That night at Mick's apartment, John got hungry, opened the refrigerator and to his amazement saw only a half a tomato and a bottle of beer. He left and awhile later there was a knock on the door. Mick opened the door and John stood there wearing a porter's uniform and behind him were carts full of bottled gefilte fish, lots of gefilte fish. 'Now,' he said, 'your refrigerator will be full.'"

Richards wrote that he thought that John was great fun to hang out with, "but as my father says, 'there's a difference between scratching your arse and tearing it to bits. . . . John was hilarious, but even by my standards he was extreme." This from one of the most self-punishing rock stars in history.

John loved music, particularly rhythm and blues, and as one of the Blues Brothers he had a hit album and was performing live in front of thousands of people. He was a rock star now. So he started hanging out with other rock stars. The problem was, as Richards points out in his book, most of them were lean, where John was very overweight, and generally in bad shape. He drank more heavily and did more drugs than most of the rockers he socialized with.

In *One Train Later*, Andy Summers, formerly of The Police, tells of a trip he and fellow band member Stewart Copeland made to Bali after touring Australia. They arrived at their hotel in the morning, changed into their swimsuits, and went out to the beach. Standing there was John Belushi, whom they had never met before. The three men introduced themselves, sat down at the beach bar, and drank a hearty breakfast. There was much clowning around, much laughter. Then they saw a poster that read that the "Special of the Day" at a local restaurant was magic mushroom omelets. Now, since all three were authorities on the subject of hallucinogenics, they immediately remembered that Balinese magic mushrooms are supposed to be the strongest in the world. They agreed that it was lunchtime. They changed and jumped into a battered old jeep that Summers had rented and drove to the restaurant.

There they had their omelettes and got back in the jeep and decided to drive to the harbor. As they drove, they commented that nothing was happening. As soon as they got into the city, they clearly saw that it was crowded with Balinese motorists driving around on Vespas. Suddenly, the magic mushrooms started to take effect and they all began to hallucinate. Summers drove the car in and out of traffic, neatly dodging pedestrians and Vespa riders, even though he was tripping. In the back, Belushi was singing and describing the colors he saw. Copeland was waving his arms and beating imaginary drums. Miraculously they drove through the city without hitting anyone and then went out to the country again. By now deeply into the magic of the mushrooms, Summers swerved the car and they landed in a ditch. As they emerged, it started to rain. The rain was South Pacific rain, which is more like floodwater coming down on you. The jeep was uncovered and they struggled to put up a temporary cover. After a half hour they realized they were so wet it didn't really matter. So all three just laid down in the mud and let the rain pour down on them. When the rain stopped, they got up, started the car again, and headed back to the hotel. On the way, they stopped to watch some Balinese soccer players kicking a ball around. At one point, the ball rolled to Belushi on the sidelines. He gave it a mighty, muddy kick and the soccer players were impressed. So, they entered the game. It was the three of them against eleven players. They ran, they kicked, they held the ball, they distorted every rule in the game of soccer, but everybody was laughing: all fourteen of them. When the game was over, wet and ragged and still hallucinating, they drove back to the hotel and passed out.

By the early 1980s John was miserably unhappy. His most recent movies had been box office failures. He had left *Saturday Night Live* and although he still toured as one of the Blues Brothers, it was not as strong an attraction as it had been. He needed a new movie and he made a deal with Paramount for them to produce a picture based on a screenplay he had cowritten. It was called *Noble Rot* and he worked it and reworked it until he thought it was good.

There are few actors who make frequent good decisions about the films they should be in, when they are the ones making that decision and not their agents or managers. Belushi had made bad decisions about *Neighbors* and *Continental Divide* and Paramount felt he was making another one in *Noble Rot*. The script just didn't work, and the film was never made.

John and I would begin to work together one more time. In early 1982, Don Simpson, then president of Paramount Pictures, called me one night and told me of an idea he had. Paramount had the rights to Alex Comfort's bestselling book *The Joy of Sex* and they didn't know what to do with it. The book was a how-to: there was no storyline. It had no characters. He wanted to do *National Lampoon's Joy of Sex,* and I had to agree: It was a great idea.

The next morning I wrote a story based on one man's adventures with sex from his childhood through his adult life. I went to Paramount and met with Michael Eisner, the head of the studio, Jeff Katzenberg, then his right-hand man, and Simpson. They approved the story and I immediately called John Hughes and told him he was writing the screenplay.

As soon as the screenplay was completed, we knew we wanted Belushi to play the leading role. He was short of money and needed a job in a hurry, and so I convinced him to take *The Joy of Sex.* John told me he hated the script, in particular the opening scene in which he played an infant in a diaper. He thought it was ridiculous. I told John that with special effects and the magic of movies it would work. He agreed to do the role.

After discussing a number of directors, Eisner came up

with Penny Marshall, the television actress, for whom this would be her first film as director. When I met with her I asked her how she'd go about it. "Well, I intend to have my ex-husband, Rob Reiner, and my friends, Steven Spielberg, Bob Zemeckis, and others come to the set almost every day and give me advice."

That sold me.

In a month we were almost finished with casting and preproduction. On March 5, 1982, I was at my home when I got the call that John Belushi had died.

I often think of John, since his death. The night he died, Jeff Greenfield, a former *Lampoon* editor, called me. He was now one of the writers and commentators on Ted Koppel's *Nightline* news show on ABC. He wanted me to appear on the show that night to talk about John. I told him I couldn't do it. I wasn't up to talking to anyone that day, much less in front of a television camera.

I have great memories of working with John, from the time we did *Lemmings*, the *National Lampoon Radio Show*, the *National Lampoon Show*, and then, of course, *Animal House*. In those three or four years, he was always a rascal but also one of the most lovable people I had ever met. He was a teddy bear who could do tricks. During *Lemmings* he would hit me up for ten- or twenty-dollar loans. He never paid them back, nor did I ever ask him to. I remember how dedicated he was during the *Radio Show* and how he brought such incredible talent to that show: Harold Ramis, Gilda Radner, Joe Flaherty, and other friends, including Harry Shearer, Paul Schaffer, Bill Murray, and Brian Doyle-Murray. When he ran the *Radio Show*, he ran it like clockwork. He followed one of the greatest humorists of our time, and the show didn't miss a beat.

When we decided to do the *National Lampoon Show*, I made him director. He was in charge. Ramis's presence was always there, advising, rewriting, but it was John who put it all together. To him, directing those two shows as well as acting in them was very important in his life because it was the first time he was in charge.

"You almost had the feeling," someone once said, "that John was going to jump off the stage and attack someone. He never did, you just felt that way."

He actually *did* jump off the stage once, but only to protect someone. During a New York performance of the *Lampoon Show*, comedian Martin Mull was sitting up front. He was drinking heavily and began to heckle the actors. Bill Murray leaped off the stage and grabbed Mull. John followed and pulled Bill away from Mull, both of whom were down on the floor under a table.

John was that way—he would always be there.

Richard Widmark offered a good definition of a star, but how do you define a legend? "A legend," as a friend of mine from the entertainment business once said, "is a star you talk about years after they die." John is still talked about and loved by so many people, who still watch *Animal House* or *Saturday Night Live* reruns. His talent was so awesome that it has stayed with us for more than thirty years, and he's a legend who will continue to stay with us.

20

LEGACY

The year after *Animal House* opened we were given the People's Choice Award for Best Comedy of 1978, and Ivan and I were named Producers of the Year.

Over the years, *Animal House* would be at the top, or high up, on every "best comedy" poll or list ever compiled. The Smithsonian named it as one of the one hundred best movies of all time. *Vanity Fair* did them one better, calling it one of the fifty best movies of all time. In polls conducted nationwide, it's been named one of the five best comedies of all time and repeatedly is listed as the best comedy ever. *Animal House* was voted number one on the Bravo channel's list of funniest movies of all time, and in the late 1990s a Harris Poll put *Animal House* at the top of the list of America's ten favorite comedies. (A movie I was to produce after *Animal House, National Lampoon's Vacation,* was voted number seven.)

The letters and phone calls that poured into the *Lampoon* in the days, weeks, months, and years that followed the opening of *Animal House* weren't like anything we'd ever seen. The *Lampoon* had a lot of breakout humor, stories, gags, and photos that people called or wrote us about, but nothing ever exploded like *Animal House*.

One of the early calls came from a young man in Seattle who asked for me. My secretary took the call and he said to her, "I wanna tell Mr. Simmons that today I saw *Animal House* for the hundredth time." At that point, this was a couple of months after it opened, so he would have had to see it something like more than one and a half times a day for that period. My assistant took his name and address and we promptly mailed him a foam pillow, an empty ice bag, and a bottle of aspirin, with a letter of congratulations.

I received this letter recently from Wade Ellis in Virginia:

I was stationed on a U.S. submarine and life can be boring/stressful. Every Saturday night at midnight we had pizza and watched Animal House. It was a great tradition and the mess decks were packed with guys cutting up and laughing.

Whenever old shipmates talk, it always includes memories of watching Animal House while under way.

I was on the USS Groton *SSN 694 out of Groton, CT. It was our 1980 deployment. When I got to the USS* Baton Rouge *SSN 689 in 1983, it was the same thing. Pizza and* Animal House!

One letter was from a fraternity member in Iowa. "Actually," he wrote, "one of our seniors has slept with the wife of a professor, not the dean's wife, but a professor's wife." We dismissed that out of hand.

We got a letter with a picture of a horse. The writer explained that he and his fratmates had indeed taken the horse one night into a lecture hall and left the animal there. "He didn't drop dead, but he dropped a load."

At the University of Oregon recently, the school's president Richard Lariviere, celebrated his sixtieth birthday. On that day, when he walked into his office—the very same office Dean Wormer used during the filming of the movie—there was his birthday present, a dead horse (not real), on the floor, on his back, stiff legs up in the air.

Not far from that office is a large boulder. On it is a bronze plaque that tells all that *Animal House* was shot on the campus.

There were hundreds of telephone calls, calls insisting that they must speak personally to Kenney or Chris Miller or Harold Ramis or me. They were so constant that we assigned an assistant to answer them. He would tell anyone who asked for any of us, "Oh, Mr. Simmons is in the hospital. But he's resting well. Nervous breakdown, you know."

We got a lot of letters from kids who said they weren't old enough to get into the theater to see the picture but had sneaked in anyway or gotten an adult to take them. One fourteen-year-old said his father had taken him and laughed louder than he did, but when they got outside the theater, his dad turned to him and said, "I don't want to hear that you do any of those things!"

The women in the movie were asked for, as well. Karen

Allen, Mary Louise Weller, Martha Smith, and Sarah Holcomb all received calls at the *Lampoon* enquiring where they could be contacted. Once again, we had a single answer: "They're all staying at the Barbizon Hotel for Women on Lexington Avenue. Please call and ask for Babs or Mandy or Clorette, but don't ask for Katy."

We actually wrote these script lines for the person assigned to answering telephone calls and correspondence. Occasionally, Doug would answer a call himself when he was in town and give even weirder answers.

I learned of an AA meeting where a particpant confessed, "I was fine, until one day I saw this movie and I got into a wild life and heavy drinking." He emphasized, "It was called *Animal House.*"

Animal House didn't merely make people laugh or start careers or make life more interesting on college campuses. It also introduced new expressions into the American lexicon. The movie was full of funny, memorable lines that have since been said and re-said, and printed and reprinted, and adapted to political situations and everyday life.

When, early in his presidency, conservatives complained that Barack Obama was keeping secrets and not letting the public know what was going on in the White House, the press called it "triple secret probation." Dean Wormer's fierce punishment was now indeed threatening the country.

Everyone has an opinion as to which is their favorite line. Well remembered and frequently repeated by on-air commentators is university founder Emil Faber's motto, "Knowledge is good." We had a number of screenings before the picture opened in order to see what was getting laughs and what wasn't, and that line brought peels of laughter within seconds of the opening sequence.

Elston Brooks of the *Fort Worth Star-Telegram* had his idea about the funniest line in the movie: "Belushi delivers the picture's most priceless line. Kicked out of school for a 0.0 grade average, he moans, 'Seven years of college down the drain.'"

Often repeated both in magazines and, even more often, in verbal bouts between friends, was Otter's assurance to Flounder that the destruction of his brother Fred's car was his own mistake. He said it this way: "You fucked up. You trusted us." Or Bluto's calm guidance to the distraught Flounder: "My advice to you is to start drinking heavily."

Lines from the movie are quoted constantly by such television and radio personalities as Keith Olbermann, Bill Maher, and many others. If *Animal House* isn't the most quoted movie of all time, it's hard to imagine what would be.

The name *Animal House* itself has become part of our language. Only recently were General Stanley McChrystal and his staff referred to by commentators as the "Animal House" for weeks after McChrystal's inappropriate remarks in *Rolling Stone* that led to his resigning his post in Afghanistan.

In June 2007, Sean Daniel had something to say about it on *The Huffington Post*:

> It has happened again and it has to end. The use of the term "Animal House" to represent foul political behavior or historical events gone very badly has got to be stopped. . . .

What really happened at *Animal House?* . . .
People of all races and religions were embraced as was
made clear when John Blutarsky welcomed freshmen
Larry Kroger and Kent Dorfman after they had been
summarily dismissed from Omega House. . . .

Any objective review must state that Maureen
Dowd, in *The New York Times* did get it right when
she wrote that President Clinton was "the first *Animal
House* President." The egalitarian beliefs that he es-
poused, the way he conducted himself and his love of
popular culture were in the proud tradition of the
Deltas.

Gail Collins, op-ed columnist of *The New York Times*,
however, devoted a column to McChrystal and his Animal
House in the issue of June 23, 2010, "General McChrystal's
Twitters." Here are some excerpts.

DAY 1

In Paris with my Kabul posse—Bluto, Otter, Boon,
Pinto, Flounder. Plus some newbie. Guys call him
Scribbles.

Collins picks it up later:

DAY 2

Stuck going to dinner with some damned French min-
ister. Gang riding me big. Bluto says they will make
me eat snails. Hell of a funny guy, Bluto.

And further on:

Night starts on a bad note. McDonald's won't let Pinto and Otter bring in the Tequiza. Damn. Wanted to show the Missus a good time. ☹

With a big ending:

• ROAD TRIP!!!!

According to a January 2011 article in the *Toronto Sun* entitled "'Rein in Animal House Frats,' Councillor Says," people are still blaming *Animal House* for frat antics. "Most of the city's twenty-four fraternities and sororities are well-behaved," it read, and the official "just wants the worst offenders to tone down their Animal House antics."

In 2008, the following, written by Christine Fall, appeared on the AMCtv.com Web site:

FIVE WAYS ANIMAL HOUSE CHANGED AMERICA

Turns out, the Delta's "futile and stupid gesture" wasn't futile at all. Thirty years after its original release, the accidental accomplishments of *Animal House* are clear:

1. Without *Animal House*, Spielberg wouldn't have known about Karen Allen. Without Karen Allen there would be no Marion Ravenwood—at least, not the one Indy fans know and love. Spielberg said having her in the role made *Raiders of the Lost Ark* "an entirely different movie." Yeah, an awesome one.

2. Did someone say toga party? Let's not pretend the movie created the idea, but it certainly popularized it, taking the idea from the White House to the frat house. First Lady Eleanor Roosevelt organized one of the first known toga parties as a way to poke fun at her husband's Caesar-like reputation. After *Animal House* came out in 1978, university students adopted the practice to escape the pressures of academia and to celebrate the movie. *Time* magazine called the new campus craze a "Bed Sheets Bonanza"; it remains a college rite of passage today.

3. Imagine life without the trivia game Six Degrees of Kevin Bacon. It all started when, as Chip Diller, Kevin Bacon pledged Omega. Getting spanked at the Omega initiation, the actor said, "Thank you, sir! May I have another?" and Hollywood said yes, yes, yes. Several roles later, college students (appropriately enough) created the game as one of their "stupid party tricks." It, in turn, inspired Kevin Bacon to create the charitable social network SixDegrees.org.

4. Jake Blues might have been born on *Saturday Night Live* but he was conceived at Faber College. No Bluto, no Blues Brothers. On a break from filming, Belushi saw blues singer Curtis Salgado at the Eugene Hotel lounge. Impressed with both the artist and the blues, he quickly went from borrowing Salgado's albums to joining him on stage. Back in New York, Belushi and Ackroyd formed the Blues Brothers Band; albums and films soon followed.

5. The film's financial success encouraged its creators to continue making ridiculous comedies. From *National Lampoon's Vacation* to John Landis's *Spies Like Us*, they kept America laughing and Chevy Chase employed. And laughter is the best medicine: Watch *Animal House* and your blood vessels will function better.

International radio and television media covered the film's twenty-fifth-anniversary celebration in August 2003. CBS reported that a reunion of the cast shut down Hollywood Boulevard. Newspapers, radio, and television carried stories and photos of the "Jackie Kennedy"–clad coeds in floats, the ROTC marchers and the stars waving from atop open convertibles and, of course, the elephant and the "Deathmobile."

"This is my college reunion." ABC quoted Peter Riegert as shouting.

In *LA Weekly*, Michael Simmons explained it in more detail:

TOGA! TOGA! TOGA!

A real live elephant plodded down the route, supplying today's prerequisite scatological humor as the keepers with shovels and garbage bags following him received hearty applause. The Deathmobile careened down Hollywood Boulevard to "disrupt" the parade and out popped a Belushi look-alike. "He should work on the eyebrows," former *Lampoon* editor/*Saturday Night Live* writer Anne Beatts said to me, referring to the stand-in's inability to replicate Belushi's facial gym-nastics. A food fight ensued between paid extras—the food made of little pink sponges—and if you're one of the few Americans who don't know what a Deathmobile or a toga party or a food fight is, rent the fucking DVD.

And so it goes. In my house we happily call *Animal House* "The movie that just won't go away." The damn movie seems to be everywhere, all the time.

"Thank you, sir! May I have another?"

Afterword:
Personal Notes

So, *Animal House* made me a film producer and for three decades people have been asking me what a producer does. I will tell you.

The screenwriter, obviously, writes the screenplay. The actors, of course, act in that screenplay. And the director, without question, directs the whole thing. But what does the producer do? A film producer is the guy who, when a writer tells him about a good idea he's got for a screenplay, says something like this.

"That was done in 1938 by William Wyler. It costarred Fredric March and Loretta Young, with Claude Rains playing the bad guy. But you know what? I think we could update it, if instead of making the leading lady a nun, we have her working in a casino in Nevada. We put George Clooney in the Fredric March role, and we make him an undercover agent for the CIA who has tracked a Russian agent to Las Vegas. Angelina Jolie would be great for the girl.

"They meet and fall in love, but he discovers that she's pregnant by the Russian agent. George has been licensed to kill this guy, who, incidentally, will be played by Jack Black, but Angelina begs George not to kill the father of her unborn child. In a tearstained scene at the Las Vegas airport, Angelina says good-bye to George and walks to the plane to join Jack Black for the trip back to Moscow. Our big ballad goes here. Maybe we get Elton John.

"George stops at the airport and pulls out a quarter—a quarter she gave him! He drops it in a slot machine. The place goes nuts—bells ringing and all that stuff. George has hit the million-dollar jackpot! He collects his money in a single large suitcase. It's all in ones to make it more visual—this is a visual medium.

"He goes back to his hotel. He's still sick about losing Angelina. He takes the million down to the hotel casino and puts the whole thing on number 27, which was their number. We see the ball rolling around and around and around, endlessly, while the theme music, sung by Celine Dion, soars until every butt in every seat is up in the air. The ball drops into number 29, then hiccups slightly and pops into 28, then, as Celine reaches a pitch so high that every dog within a mile of any moviehouse in America is howling with pain, the ball goes *blip* and drops into 27."

By now, the writer, who's on the edge of his seat listening to the producer, is ecstatic. "And Angelina returns to him!" he screams.

"No," says the producer. "That's what would have happened in 1938. Instead we go for total realism. George meets two bimbos, played by Britney Spears and Paris Hilton, buys champagne for everybody in Las Vegas, and sends a telegram to Angelina, which she receives as she and Jack Black land in Moscow. It reads simply '#*%! you!' in Russian.

"As we go out on a big rock number by Bon Jovi, George is buying a training bra with diamond studs on it for Paris, and Britney gets the last big laugh of the movie by falling up a down escalator."

"I love it!" says the writer, leaping from his seat. He drives like a maniac back home and writes a first draft overnight, and the producer takes it to one of the studios.

There, a reader who occupies a small closetlike office in a building near the parking lot and drinks from a *Star Wars* mug reads it and condenses it to about a page and a half. Finally, because this is from a prestigious producer, it wends its way through numerous assistants and production vice presidents, and, on the big day, the producer arrives to meet the head of the studio.

The head man, who hasn't read the screenplay or the condensed version but does know who has been suggested for the leading roles, because that's more important than the script, says, "George Clooney is in the dumper. Angelina's fine, and the kids like Jack Black. We want Brad Pitt for the guy and Ashton Kutcher for the girl's kid brother."

The producer doesn't remember that there is a kid brother, but he's on a roll, so why argue? He agrees to the casting.

"And," says the head of the studio, "we want Steven Spielberg to direct. We've already contacted him and he says as long as you stay off the set, he'll do it."

The producer then negotiates his own deal, taking an exceedingly large piece of the pie, flies to Bimini, where his yacht has been moored for the winter, and for the next six months sails around the Greek islands with Kim Kardashian and her mother.

The picture is made and released, is a huge hit, and garners no Oscar nominations. The producer makes millions, leaves his yacht in Greece, flies back to America, and buys another one.

It's that easy.

Index